OFFICIAL SQA PAST PAPERS WITH ANSWERS

KU-178-137

## STANDARD GRADE | FOUNDATION | GENERAL

# ENGLISH
# 2006-2009

© Scottish Qualifications Authority

First exam published in 2006.
Published by Bright Red Publishing Ltd, 6 Stafford Street, Edinburgh EH3 7AU
tel: 0131 220 5804 fax: 0131 220 6710 info@brightredpublishing.co.uk  www.brightredpublishing.co.uk

ISBN 978-1-84948-010-9

A CIP Catalogue record for this book is available from the British Library.

Bright Red Publishing is grateful to the copyright holders, as credited on the final page of the book, for permission to use their material. Every effort has been made to trace the copyright holders and to obtain their permission for the use of copyright material. Bright Red Publishing will be happy to receive information allowing us to rectify any error or omission in future editions.

STANDARD GRADE | FOUNDATION

# 2006
## READING

[BLANK PAGE]

F

# 0860/401

| NATIONAL QUALIFICATIONS 2006 | WEDNESDAY, 3 MAY 10.35 AM – 11.25 AM | ENGLISH STANDARD GRADE Foundation Level Reading Text |

Read carefully the passage overleaf.  It will help if you read it twice.  When you have done so, answer the questions.  Use the spaces provided in the Question/Answer booklet.

SCOTTISH
QUALIFICATIONS
AUTHORITY

©

# Ain't no mountain high enough

Scott Cory is only 14 but he's already scaled some of the highest, most dangerous rock-faces in the world. **Deborah Netburn** watches "Spider-Boy" in action in California.

1  As she stands in the valley of Yosemite National Park, northern California, Jennifer Cory stares intently through a high-powered telescope trained at a great wall of forbidding grey granite which juts high above the alpine meadow. Though she may look like a devoted bird-watcher, the dark-haired 38-year-old is actually keeping a close eye on her 14-year-old son, the American rock-climbing sensation Scott Cory, who is scaling the 2,900 ft wall. High above his mother, the sandy-haired boy keeps his body pressed close against the wall as he calmly scans the rock for the next tiny nick to use as a hand or foot hold. He makes his way quickly and methodically up the great wall. When at last he comes to a pitch (a small ledge to use as a resting place) he stops and calmly looks down at the forest landscape a full skyscraper's length below him. "He looks just as comfortable as if he was standing in his own front yard," says his mother.

2  This trip to Yosemite, two hours from the Corys' home just north of San Francisco, is part of Scott's training for two rock-climbing feats he has planned for the summer. This week he will climb El Capitan and Half Dome. Then, in August, Scott and his fellow rock-climber Steve Schneider, 43, will fly to Lima, Peru, where they plan to be the first Americans to climb "Welcome to the Slabs of Koricancha", a 2,000 ft near-vertical route up La Esfinge mountain. What makes this climb particularly difficult, besides the few hand and foot holds, is the high altitude. The base of the route is 14,000 ft. But Scott seems unconcerned. "It looks like a lot of fun," he tells me.

3  Although Scott hasn't entered high school yet, he has all the trappings of a sports superstar: a sponsorship clothing deal that he picked up at the age of seven; his own sports agent (who also represents Anna Kournikova); and a lot of media coverage (he's appeared on TV and in *Sports Illustrated* in America). Thanks to his good looks he is also starting to build a female fanbase: in one web chatroom a teenage girl listed him as one of her three favourite stars along with Orlando Bloom and Johnny Depp.

4  Scott, who started climbing on a family holiday when he was 7, set his first record when he was 11 by becoming the youngest person to climb "The Nose" of El Capitan, one of the world's most famous and difficult climbing routes. One month later he became the youngest person to do the climb in one day. Fellow rock-climbers say they admire the dedication that has kept this 14-year-old in the gym for four days a week, five hours a day for the past seven years.

5  "I think what sets Scotty apart from a lot of kids," says Beth Rodden, 23, a climber who has known Scott since he was seven, "is that he is up for any challenge, and that is really the key to his success."

6  Scott's explanation of what keeps him in the gym instead of in front of a PlayStation is simple and short. "I love it, and it's fun for me."

7  Indeed, away from the rock-face, in a café down the street from the University of California at Berkeley, Scott looks and acts entirely his age.

8  At the café, Scott is joined by his "mom" Jennifer, and his dad, Jim.

9  Scott orders a pizza, but when it comes he sends it back because the chef has forgotten to hold the anchovies. To tide him over the waitress brings a small leek and onion tart.

10  Scott eyes the tart suspiciously.

11  "Try it," says his mother.

Scott Cory climbing in Red Rocks, Nevada

2    "You try it, Dad," says Scott, moving the plate closer to his father.

3    An hour later he is back in his element at the Touchstone rock-climbing gym at Mission Cliffs in San Francisco. Gyms like these are becoming increasingly popular in the United States; in the early 1990s there were around five, today there are over 500. Scott bounds through the glass doors, nods hello to a man working at the front desk, and steps into a harness. He clips on a little satchel containing powdery chalk to keep his hands dry, and pulls on a tiny pair of rock-climbing shoes.

4    "Scott usually wears a size nine but those shoes are six and a half," observes his father. "He crams his toes in there so he can feel every little thing when he is climbing the wall."

5    Within ten minutes Scott is moving swiftly up the artificial rock-face. The press has nicknamed him "Spider-Boy" because of his technique, though he says nobody calls him that in real life. But the nickname is good—the way he holds his body parallel to the wall, the way he makes full use of the span of his arms and legs, the trail of rope he leaves behind him as he climbs. In the gym, where he is able to study the routes from the ground, his climbing is more graceful than it is on the mountain.

16    Scott is still unsure what sort of future he will have in rock-climbing.

17    "I think he would love to see himself climbing for a living, but it just isn't a big enough sport," says his mother. "The professional climbers he knows just get by on a measly existence, but he hasn't even entered high school yet, so we have to see what happens. He could decide tomorrow that he doesn't like it anymore. Although I don't think anyone imagines that will happen."

18    Back on the wall Scott works on the final section of the hardest route. Grasping the small rubber holds he swiftly moves upwards. Below, his friends in the gym cheer for him, but just as he reaches the top his hand slips and he is left dangling in the air.

19    Scott has been here three hours already, and he has tried this particular route at least five times. His parents are ready to leave but Scott won't hear of it. He isn't going anywhere until he gets it right.

Adapted from the
*Sunday Telegraph Magazine*

[*END OF PASSAGE*]

**[BLANK PAGE]**

FOR OFFICIAL USE

Total Mark

**F**

# 0860/402

NATIONAL
QUALIFICATIONS
2006

WEDNESDAY, 3 MAY
10.35 AM – 11.25 AM

ENGLISH
STANDARD GRADE
Foundation Level
Reading
Questions

---

**Fill in these boxes and read what is printed below.**

Full name of centre

Town

Forename(s)

Surname

Date of birth

Day  Month  Year    Scottish candidate number    Number of seat

**NB Before leaving the examination room you must give this booklet to the invigilator. If you do not, you may lose all the marks for this paper.**

SCOTTISH
QUALIFICATIONS
AUTHORITY

SA 0860/401 6/32070

*Marks*

## QUESTIONS

**Write your answers in the spaces provided.**

**Look at Paragraph 1.**

1.  Where **exactly** in northern California is Jennifer Cory as she watches her son climb?

    _____        2   1   0

2.  Write down the expression which suggests that Jennifer is concentrating very hard on what she is doing.

    _____        2   ■   0

3.  "Though she may look like a devoted bird-watcher . . ."

    Give a reason why Jennifer could be mistaken for a bird-watcher.

    _____        2   ■   0

4.  ". . . a great wall of forbidding grey granite . . ."

    What impression do we get of the mountain from this description?

    _____        2   1   0

5.  **Write down three separate words** the writer uses in Paragraph 1 to suggest Scott Cory is a good climber.

    [        ]        [        ]        [        ]        2   1   0

6.  ". . . **a full skyscraper's length below him**"

    Explain fully why the writer uses this expression here.

    _____

    _____        2   1   0

PAGE
TOTAL

*Marks*

**Look at Paragraph 2.**

7. "'It looks like a lot of fun,' he tells me."

    Give **two** reasons why the reader might find Scott's statement surprising.

    (i) _____  2 ■ 0

    (ii) _____  2 ■ 0

**Look at Paragraph 3.**

8. (*a*) Give **three** pieces of evidence that show Scott ". . . has all the trappings of a sports superstar".

    _____

    _____  2 1 0

    (*b*) Why are the words *Sports Illustrated* in italics?

    _____  2 ■ 0

**Look at Paragraph 4.**

9. What were the first **two** climbing records which Scott set?

    (i) _____  2 1 0

    (ii) _____  2 1 0

10. Write down **one word** from which **sums up** Scott's attitude to training.

    ┌─────────────────────┐
    │                     │
    └─────────────────────┘  2 ■ 0

**[Turn over**

*Marks*

**Look at Paragraphs 7 to 12.**

**11.** Why does the writer put inverted commas around "mom"?

_____    2 ■ 0

**12.** In the café, how does Scott behave like a typical teenager?

_____

_____    2 1 0

**Look at Paragraphs 13 and 14.**

**13.** What evidence does the writer give to show that rock climbing gyms ". . . are becoming increasingly popular" (Paragraph 13)?

_____    2 1 0

**14. Write down an expression** from Paragraph 13 which suggests Scott is eager to begin training.

_____    2 ■ 0

**15.** (*a*)  Why does Scott have to "cram" his toes into his rock-climbing shoes?

_____    2 ■ 0

(*b*)  What does he gain from doing this?

_____    2 ■ 0

PAGE
TOTAL

*Marks*

**Look at Paragraph 15.**

**16.** (*a*)   "The press has nicknamed him Spider-Boy . . ."

Tick (✓) the **three best** reasons why, **according to the passage**, this is a good nickname.

His rope looks like a spider's thread. ☐

He is very young. ☐

He looks like a character from a comic. ☐

He uses his arms and legs at full stretch. ☐

He holds his body at the same angle as the wall. ☐

He is climbing indoors. ☐

2  1  0

(*b*)   Which expression, **used later in the passage**, reminds the reader of this comparison with a spider?

_____

2  ■  0

**Look at Paragraphs 16 and 17.**

**17.  Write down an expression** which suggests that some professional climbers do not make much money from the sport.

_____

2  ■  0

**Look at Paragraphs 18 and 19.**

**18.** What **two** pieces of evidence show that Scott does not like to give up on a climb?

_____

_____

2  1  0

**[Turn over for Question 19 on *Page six***

PAGE
TOTAL

*Marks*

**Think about the passage as a whole.**

**19.** (*a*) What impression do you, as a reader, get of Scott Cory?

_____  2 ■ 0

(*b*) Give **two** pieces of evidence from the passage to support your answer.

_____

_____  2 1 0

[*END OF QUESTION PAPER*]

PAGE
TOTAL

# STANDARD GRADE | GENERAL

# 2006
## READING

[BLANK PAGE]

**G**

# 0860/403

| | | |
|---|---|---|
| NATIONAL QUALIFICATIONS 2006 | WEDNESDAY, 3 MAY 1.00 PM – 1.50 PM | **ENGLISH STANDARD GRADE** General Level Reading Text |

Read carefully the passage overleaf. It will help if you read it twice. When you have done so, answer the questions. Use the spaces provided in the Question/Answer booklet.

SCOTTISH
QUALIFICATIONS
AUTHORITY

©

*In this extract from a novel set in a secondary school, the narrator, John, is sitting in his Maths class. Gloria (nicknamed Glory Hallelujah) is another pupil in the same class.*

1　I am sitting in school, in Maths, with a piece of paper in my hand. No, it is not my algebra homework. It is not a quiz that I have finished and am waiting to hand in to Mrs Moonface. The piece of paper in my hand has nothing at all to do with Mathematics. Nor does it have to do with any school subject. Nor is it really a piece of paper at all.

2　It is really my fate, masquerading as paper.

3　I am sitting next to Glory Hallelujah and I am waiting for a break in the action. Mrs Moonface is at the front of the room, going on about integers. I am not hearing a single thing that she is saying. She could stop lecturing about integers and start doing a cancan kick or singing a rap song and I would not notice.

4　She could call on me and ask me any question on earth, and I would not be able to answer.

5　But luckily, she does not call on me. She has a piece of chalk in her right hand. She is waving it around like a dagger as she spews algebra gibberish at a hundred miles a minute.

6　I hear nothing. Algebra does not have the power to penetrate my feverish isolation.

7　You see, I am preparing to ask Glory Hallelujah out on a date.

8　I am on an island, even though I am sitting at my desk surrounded by my classmates.

9　I am on Torture Island.

10　There are no trees on Torture Island—no huts, no hills, no beaches. There is only doubt.

11　Gloria will laugh at me. That thought is my lonely and tormenting company here on Torture Island. The exact timing and nature of her laughter are open to endless speculation.

12　She may not take me seriously. Her response may be "Oh, John, do you exist? Are you here on earth with me? I wasn't aware we were sharing the same universe."

13　Or she may be even more sarcastic. "John, I would love to go on a date with you, but I'm afraid I have to change my cat's litter box that night ."

14　So, as you can see, Torture Island is not exactly a beach resort. I am not having much fun here. I am ready to seize my moment and leave Torture Island forever.

15　In registration, I ripped a piece of paper from my yellow notepad. My black ball-point pen shook slightly in my trembling right hand as I wrote out the fateful question: "Gloria, will you go out with me this Friday?" Beneath that monumental question, I drew two boxes. One box was conspicuously large. I labelled it the YES box. The second box was tiny. I labelled it the NO box.

16　And that is the yellow piece of paper I have folded up into a square and am holding in my damp hand as I wait here on Torture Island for Mrs Moonface to turn towards the blackboard and give me the opportunity I need.

17　I cannot approach Glory Hallelujah after class because she is always surrounded by her friends. I cannot wait and pass the note to her later in the week because she may make plans to go out with one of her girlfriends. No, it is very evident to me that today is the day, and that I must pass the note before this period ends or forever live a coward.

18    There are only ten minutes left in Maths and Mrs Moonface seems to have no intention of recording her algebraic observations for posterity. Perhaps the piece of yellow chalk in her hand is just a prop. It is possible that the previous night she hurt her wrist in an arm-wrestling competition and can no longer write. It is also possible that she has forgotten all about her pupils and believes that she is playing a part in a Hollywood movie.

19    There are only seven minutes left in Maths. I attempt to turn Mrs Moonface towards the blackboard by telekinesis. The atoms of her body prove remarkably resistant to my telepathic powers.

20    There are six minutes left. Now there are five.

21    Mrs Moonface, for Pete's sake, write something on the blackboard! That is what Mathematics teachers do! Write down axioms, simplify equations, draw rectangles, measure angles, even, if you must, sketch the sneering razor-toothed face of Algebra itself. WRITE ANYTHING!

22    Suddenly Mrs Moonface stops lecturing.

23    Her right hand, holding the chalk, rises.

24    Then her hips begin to pivot.

25    This all unfolds in very slow motion. The sheer importance of the moment slows the action way, way down.

26    The pivoting of Mrs Moonface's hips causes a corresponding rotation in the plane of her shoulders and upper torso.

27    Her neck follows her shoulders, as day follows night.

28    Eventually, the lunar surface of her face is pulled towards the blackboard.

29    She begins to write. I have no idea what she is writing. It could be hieroglyphics and I would not notice. It could be a map to Blackbeard's treasure and I would not care.

30    I am now primed. My heart is thumping against my ribs, one by one, like a hammer pounding out a musical scale on a metal keyboard. Bing. Bang. Bong. Bam. I am breathing so quickly that I cannot breathe, if that makes any sense.

31    I am aware of every single one of my classmates in Maths.

32    Everyone in Maths is now preoccupied. There are only four minutes left in the period. Mrs Moonface is filling up blackboard space at an unprecedented speed, no doubt trying to scrape every last kernel of mathematical knowledge from the corncob of her brain before the bell. My classmates are racing to keep up with her. All around me pens are moving across notebooks at such a rate that ink can barely leak out and affix itself to paper.

33    My moment is at hand! The great clapper in the bell of fate clangs for me! *Ka-wang! Ka-wang!*

34    My right hand rises and begins to move sideways, very slowly, like a submarine, travelling at sub-desk depth to avoid teacher radar.

35    My right index finger makes contact with the sacred warm left wrist of Glory Hallelujah!

36    She looks down to see who is touching her at sub-desk depth. Spots my hand, with its precious yellow note.

37    Gloria understands instantly.

38    The exchange of the covert note is completed in a nanoinstant. Mrs Moonface and the rest of our Maths class have no idea that anything momentous has taken place.

39    I reverse the speed and direction of my right hand, and it returns safely to port.

40    Gloria has transferred my note to her lap and has moved her right elbow to block anyone on that side of her from seeing. The desk itself provides added shielding.

41    In the clever safe haven that she has created, she unfolds my note. Reads it.

42    She does not need to speak. She does not need to check the YES or NO boxes on my note. If she merely blinks, I will understand. If she wrinkles her nose, the import of her nose wrinkle will not be lost on me. In fact, so total is my concentration in that moment of grand suspense I am absolutely positive that there is nothing that Glory Hallelujah can do, no reaction that she can give off, that I will not immediately and fully understand.

43    I would stake my life on it.

44    But what she does do is this. She folds my note back up. Without looking at me—without even an eye blink or a nose wrinkle—she raises it to her lips. For one wild instant I think that she is going to kiss it.

45    Her pearly teeth part.

46    She eats my note.

Adapted from the novel *"You Dont Know Me"* By David Klass

[*END OF PASSAGE*]

FOR OFFICIAL USE

**G**

Total Mark

# 0860/404

NATIONAL QUALIFICATIONS 2006

WEDNESDAY, 3 MAY 1.00 PM – 1.50 PM

ENGLISH
STANDARD GRADE
General Level
Reading
Questions

**Fill in these boxes and read what is printed below.**

Full name of centre

Town

Forename(s)

Surname

Date of birth
Day  Month  Year

Scottish candidate number

Number of seat

**NB  Before leaving the examination room you must give this booklet to the invigilator. If you do not, you may lose all the marks for this paper.**

SCOTTISH
QUALIFICATIONS
AUTHORITY

©

*Marks*

## QUESTIONS

**Write your answers in the spaces provided.**

**Look at Paragraphs 1 to 4.**

1. (*a*) Who is Mrs Moonface?

_____   2 ■ 0

(*b*) Why do you think John gives her the nickname "Mrs Moonface"?

_____

_____   2 1 0

2. "It is really my fate, masquerading as paper."

Why does the writer place this sentence in a paragraph of its own?

_____

_____   2 1 0

3. "Mrs Moonface is at the front of the room, going on about integers."

What does the expression "going on" suggest about John's attitude to what Mrs Moonface is saying?

_____   2 ■ 0

**Look at Paragraphs 5 to 10.**

4. How does the writer make Mrs Moonface's behaviour seem threatening?

_____

_____   2 1 0

PAGE
TOTAL

Marks

5. ". . . spews algebra gibberish at a hundred miles a minute. . ." (Paragraph 5)

   **Explain in your own words** what the writer's word choice in this expression suggests about what John thinks of:

   (i)  **what** she is saying;

   _____

   _____    2 ■ 0

   (ii) **how** she says it.

   _____

   _____    2 ■ 0

6. ". . . I am preparing to ask Glory Hallelujah out on a date." (Paragraph 7)

   Why do you think the writer waits until this point to reveal what John is planning to do?

   _____

   _____    2 1 0

7. "I am on Torture Island." (Paragraph 9)

   (a) **Explain fully in your own words** what the narrator means by this.

   _____

   _____    2 1 0

   (b) Write down an expression from later in the passage which contains a similar idea.

   ┌─────────────────────────────────┐
   │                                 │
   │                                 │    2 ■ 0
   └─────────────────────────────────┘

   **[Turn over**

PAGE TOTAL

*Marks*

**8.** Explain how the writer emphasises the bleakness of "Torture Island".

_____

_____    2  1  0

**Look at Paragraphs 11 to 14.**

   **9.** (*a*) **Write down an example** of the writer's use of humour in these paragraphs.

   _____

   _____    2  ■  0

   (*b*) Explain why your chosen example is funny.

   _____

   _____    2  1  0

**Look at Paragraphs 15 to 17.**

**10. Write down three** pieces of evidence that suggest the narrator's nervousness at this point in the story.

   _____

   _____

   _____    2  1  0

**11.** Quote **two** separate words used by the writer to suggest the importance of what John is asking Gloria.

   [                    ]        [                    ]    2  1  0

**12.** "One box was conspicuously large . . . The second box was tiny." (Paragraph 15)

   Why do you think John makes the boxes different sizes?

   _____

   _____    2  1  0

[  ]
PAGE
TOTAL

*Page four*

*Marks*

13. **In your own words**, give a reason why John must make his approach to Gloria during Maths.

_____

_____     2 | 1 | 0

**Look at Paragraphs 18 to 21.**

14. How does the writer suggest the mood of increasing tension at this point in the passage?

_____

_____     2 | ■ | 0

15. "WRITE ANYTHING!" (Paragraph 21)

    Why are these words written in capital letters?

_____

_____     2 | ■ | 0

**Look at Paragraphs 22 to 33**

16. (*a*)  Identify any **one** technique used by the writer in this section to suggest John's growing excitement.

    _____     2 | ■ | 0

    (*b*)  Explain **how** it does so.

    _____

    _____     2 | 1 | 0

[**Turn over for Questions 17 to 20 on** *Page six*

PAGE
TOTAL

*Marks*

**Look at Paragraphs 34 to 46.**

17. Give **three** reasons why Mrs Moonface is unaware of the note being passed.

_____

_____

_____    2  1  0

18. Why does John feel the "YES" or "NO" boxes on his note are now irrelevant?

_____

_____    2  1  0

19. How does the final paragraph provide an effective end to the passage?

_____

_____    2  1  0

**Now look at the passage as a whole.**

20. How realistic do you find the writer's description of this classroom incident? Give reasons for your opinion.

_____

_____

_____    2  1  0

*[END OF QUESTION PAPER]*

PAGE
TOTAL

# STANDARD GRADE | FOUNDATION

# 2007
## READING

[BLANK PAGE]

**F**

# 0860/401

| | | |
|---|---|---|
| NATIONAL QUALIFICATIONS 2007 | TUESDAY, 1 MAY 10.35 AM – 11.25 AM | **ENGLISH STANDARD GRADE** Foundation Level Reading Text |

Read carefully the passage overleaf. It will help if you read it twice. When you have done so, answer the questions. Use the spaces provided in the Question/Answer booklet.

# Why dumped dog is such a lucky hound

No one wanted greyhound Pal after he was abandoned for not being fast enough on the track—until an animal trainer was asked to find a dog to star in a film. DAVID WIGG tells how the renamed Celt so nearly lost out again—before finding a new home and some much-needed love.

1   As Celt the greyhound comes bounding over to me on green fields overlooking the picturesque fields of Kent, he obviously knows he is a dog in a million. Once abandoned, he is now the star of a heartwarming film.

2   Celt, with his golden fawn markings, is one of many unwanted greyhounds in Britain that are dumped if they don't come up to racing standards.

3   He had ended up being abandoned at a greyhound rescue centre. As the weeks went by, no one came to adopt Celt as a family pet but then something even more exciting happened to him.

4   Animal handler Sue Potter had been asked to find an appealing greyhound to star in the film entitled "The Mighty Celt", a touching story about a boy and his love and devotion for a dog he desperately wants to own.

5   Sue had the almost impossible task of choosing one greyhound from more than 100 at the kennels.

6   But when she saw Celt, or Pal, as he was then known, Sue immediately knew he was the one she could train for the film. So what was so special about Celt?

7   "His colouring was perfect, he had to be fawn with some white markings," says Sue. "He also had to be obedient and compatible with people and other animals.

8   "I tested his reaction to sound and that

was fine. There couldn't be anything wrong with him—he had to be an entire dog."

9   Sue trained Celt for two weeks at her home in the north of England, in preparation for his starring role. Celt then spent eight weeks filming in Northern Ireland with the cast and crew.

10   From all accounts, Celt excelled himself on set and everyone fell in love with him, but after the filming there was one big question remaining—what was to become of Celt? After all the attention he had received, it didn't seem right that he should go back to being alone and unwanted once again at the kennels, but Sue felt she couldn't keep him as she already owned five dogs.

11   Urgent inquiries were made among the crew and cast but it seemed no one was able to take him on from the film set where he had been thoroughly pampered.

12   On hearing of the young dog's plight, Kent landowner and farmer Philip Daubeny came to the rescue. Philip is chairman of the London-based charity Dogs Trust, which cares for more than 12,500 strays each year.

13   He had recently lost his own pet greyhound Tocki, another rescued dog. To everyone's relief he agreed to adopt Celt and take him to his lovely country home surrounded by 500 acres of open

hills and farmland near Maidstone. Here Celt now enjoys long walks and romps with Philip's other pets—corgis Dusty and Yehudi and five cats.

14 With Celt looking a picture of contentment, fully spread out in an armchair, Philip recalls: "The first I heard of him was through a vet in Northern Ireland called Rose McIlrath.

15 "One of her friends, Claire Millar, was working as a teacher with the children on the film. When it turned out that no real provision had been made for what was going to happen to Celt, Claire asked Rose if she had any ideas.

16 "Rose immediately thought of me because I had recently lost Tocki, who had been with me for seven years." Philip felt there was one important question that had to be asked before he agreed to take on Celt.

17 How did the greyhound get on with cats? "I was concerned because, on the whole, greyhounds are well known for chasing small furry animals, either cats or small dogs, often mistaking them for the hare on the track. I didn't want some terrible tragedy to happen with my five cats.

18 "I was assured that, after coming back to this country, Celt had been living with cats in a temporary home and I was assured of his character and that he would make a wonderful pet."

19 It was then arranged for Celt to be shipped over to the Dogs Trust Kenilworth Rehoming Centre, in Warwickshire. There he was thoroughly checked over.

20 Celt was driven down in an animal ambulance from Warwickshire to his new home in Kent in July last year.

21 "He was slightly anxious but he quickly settled down. We let him out in the field to meet the other dogs. He got on immediately with them and was keener to play with them than they were with him. He fitted in very easily and quickly, and made himself at home by sitting on every chair he could.

22 "He also wanted to jump on the beds as well, but there isn't much room to sleep if you have a greyhound on board. People think greyhounds need a lot of exercise but, actually, there's nothing they like more than curling up in an armchair and watching television."

23 I couldn't help wondering if, having been pampered on set, Celt acted like a film star. The response was laughter as Philip recalls: "He was very active and bursting with energy.

24 "At first, he rushed around as if he were on a greyhound track but, otherwise, he was among the more likeable and less affected film stars.

25 "Most affectionate, very beautiful and a genuine, kind, loving dog, that is marvellous with children."

26 Dog trainer Sue Potter adds: "I didn't want to take Celt back to the kennels because he had had a life of luxury on the film. I asked around if anyone would like to adopt him. The young boy in the film, Tyrone, fancied having him, but his father was moving house so he said no.

27 "I wanted him to go to a nice home—and he couldn't have gone to a better one. He was very lucky because he really has fallen on his feet."

Adapted from an article by David Wigg

[END OF PASSAGE]

[BLANK PAGE]

FOR OFFICIAL USE

**F**

Total Mark

# 0860/402

| NATIONAL QUALIFICATIONS 2007 | TUESDAY, 1 MAY 10.35 AM – 11.25 AM | ENGLISH STANDARD GRADE Foundation Level Reading Questions |
|---|---|---|

**Fill in these boxes and read what is printed below.**

Full name of centre

Town

Forename(s)

Surname

Date of birth
Day Month Year

Scottish candidate number

Number of seat

**NB Before leaving the examination room you must give this booklet to the invigilator. If you do not, you may lose all the marks for this paper.**

SCOTTISH QUALIFICATIONS AUTHORITY

©

*Marks*

## QUESTIONS

**Write your answers in the spaces provided.**

**Look at the Introduction and Paragraphs 1 to 3.**

1. (a) Write down **one** word from Paragraph 1 which suggests that Celt the greyhound is a fit and healthy dog.

   [ ]

   2 ■ 0

   (b) Write down an expression from Paragraph 1 which suggests that this might not always have been the case.

   [ ]

   2 ■ 0

2. ". . . don't come up to racing standards." (Paragraph 2)

   Write down an expression from the introduction to the passage which contains a similar idea.

   _____

   2 ■ 0

**Look at Paragraphs 4 and 5.**

3. ". . . a touching story about a boy and his love and devotion for a dog" (Paragraph 4)

   Tick (✔) the box beside the best definition of "touching" as it is used in this sentence.

   | | |
   |---|---|
   | exciting | |
   | true | |
   | fictional | |
   | moving | |

   2 ■ 0

*Marks*

**4.** ". . . the almost impossible task . . ." (Paragraph 5)

Why was Sue Potter's task so difficult?

_____     2 | 1 | 0

**Look at Paragraphs 6 to 8.**

**5.** Write down any **three** qualities Celt needed to have if he was to become a film star.

_____

_____

_____     2 | 1 | 0

**Look at Paragraphs 9 to 11.**

**6.** Tick (✔) the appropriate box to show whether the following statements are **True, False**, or **Cannot tell from the passage**.

|  | True | False | Cannot Tell |
|---|---|---|---|
| Sue trained Celt in Northern Ireland. |  |  |  |
| Celt spent more time being filmed than being trained. |  |  |  |
| Celt did well on the film set. |  |  |  |
| Sue Potter owns two cats. |  |  |  |

2 ■ 0

2 ■ 0

2 ■ 0

2 ■ 0

**7.** Why does the writer use a **dash (—)** in the first sentence of Paragraph 10?

_____     2 | 1 | 0

**8.** Write down an expression which suggests that Celt had been very well cared for during filming.

_____     2 ■ 0

**[Turn over**

PAGE TOTAL

*Marks*

**Look at Paragraphs 12 to 14.**

9.  Give **three** reasons why Philip Daubeny was a suitable person to rescue Celt.

_____

_____

_____    2 1 0

**Look at Paragraphs 15 to 18.**

10.  ". . . , Claire Millar, was working as a teacher with the children on the film."
     (Paragraph 15)

     Why do you think the children on the film needed a teacher?

     _____    2 1 0

11.  (*a*)  Why was Philip Daubeny concerned for the safety of his cats?

     _____

     _____    2 1 0

     (*b*)  "I didn't want some terrible tragedy to happen with my five cats."
          (Paragraph 17)

          Identify **two** techniques used in this sentence to emphasise his concern.

          _____    2 1 0

     (*c*)  Do you think "tragedy" is a good word to use here?  Give a reason.

          _____    2 ■ 0

PAGE
TOTAL

Marks

12. ". . . had been living with cats in a temporary home . . ." (Paragraph 18)

Tick (✓) the box beside the best definition of "temporary" as it is used in this sentence.

| | |
|---|---|
| long-lasting | |
| short-term | |
| animal | |
| caring | |

2  ■  0

**Look at Paragraphs 19 to 22.**

13. Give **two** pieces of evidence which show how Celt "fitted in very easily". (Paragraph 21)

_____

_____

2  1  0

14. What might some people find surprising about greyhounds?

_____

_____

2  1  0

**Look at Paragraphs 23 to 27.**

15. How does the structure of the sentence in Paragraph 25 emphasise Celt's good points?

_____

2  ■  0

16. Why was the young boy in the film unable to adopt Celt?

_____

2  1  0

**[Turn over for Questions 17 to 19 on *Page six***

PAGE
TOTAL

*Marks*

17. In what way had Celt "fallen on his feet" (Paragraph 27)?

_____

_____   2  1  0

**Think about the passage as a whole.**

18. Who do you think this passage is written for?  Tick (✔) **one** box.

| | |
|---|---|
| Film students | |
| Vets | |
| General readers | |
| Dog breeders | |

2  ■  0

19. "Why dumped dog is such a lucky hound"

Identify **two** techniques which help to make this a good title.

_____

_____   2  1  0

*[END OF QUESTION PAPER]*

PAGE
TOTAL

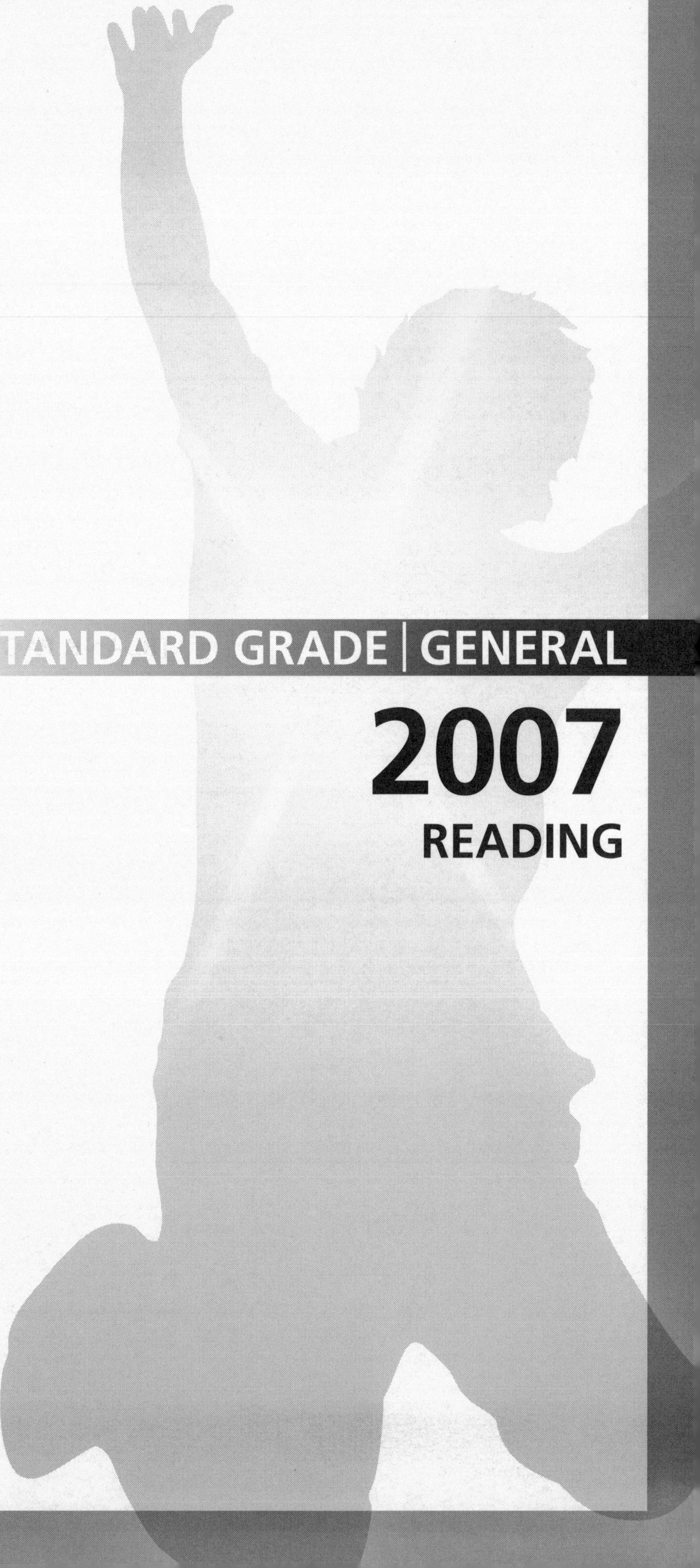

STANDARD GRADE | GENERAL

# 2007

## READING

[BLANK PAGE]

**G**

# 0860/403

| | | |
|---|---|---|
| NATIONAL QUALIFICATIONS 2007 | TUESDAY, 1 MAY 1.00 PM – 1.50 PM | **ENGLISH STANDARD GRADE** General Level Reading Text |

Read carefully the passage overleaf. It will help if you read it twice. When you have done so, answer the questions. Use the spaces provided in the Question/Answer booklet.

SCOTTISH QUALIFICATIONS AUTHORITY

©

# Biker Boys and Girls

There is only one "wall of death" doing the rounds at British fairs today. But a new generation of daredevil riders is intent on keeping the show on (or rather, off) the road.

1    Last year Kerri Cameron, aged 19 and a little bored with her job as a horse-riding instructor, was looking up job vacancies on the internet. Puzzled, she turned to her mother and said, "Mum, what's a wall of death?"

2    Her mother, Denise, a health worker who has always had a horror of motorcycles, told her that walls of death were places where people rode motorbikes round the insides of a 20 ft-high wooden drum and tried not to fall off and get killed. "Gosh," said Kerri, "that sounds fun."

3    She picked up her mobile, phoned the number mentioned on the internet and then arranged to see Ken Fox, owner of the wall of death. Ken Fox didn't ask about her school qualifications, only if she wanted a ride on the back of his bike around the wall. Yes, she said.

4    Ken Fox revved up the demonstration bike and spun it on to the 45-degree wooden apron that bridges the ground and the perpendicular wall and then took it three or four times around the lower bits of the wall itself just to see if she could cope. Then he went round with Kerri sitting on the handlebars. She passed that test, too. She thought it was fantastic. Unbelievable. The best!

5    A year later Kerri is doing 20 shows a day, driving a skeletal aluminium go-kart around Ken Fox's wall of death to within six inches of the safety wire at the top—the wire that's there to prevent the machines sailing off into the crowd. "It's much more fun than helping kids on horses," she says, giggling nervously and brushing a strand of blonde hair back behind her ear. "The only thing I really miss about home is flush toilets."

6    Ken Fox and his wife Julie, their sons, Luke and Alex, and their troupe of Kerri, a new girl rider called Emma Starr, a man who prefers to be known just as Philip, and a wall-of-death enthusiast of an accountant named Neil Calladine, now operate the last wall of death in business in Britain. Calladine is the wall's "spieler", stalking the front of the attraction with a microphone, promising thrills and excitement as Ken and Luke Fox sit on their bikes, creating the roaring throttle noises of impending danger. Later, Luke and his father dip and zig-zag their bikes across each other, spinning round the drum every four seconds, as the holiday crowds peer tentatively down over the safety wire and then, in the traditional way, shower coins into the ring after being told that wall-of-death riders can never get insurance. Each show lasts 20 minutes; at one stage four riders are zipping up, down and all around.

7    In the 1930s and 1940s there were almost 30 walls of death at seaside resorts and fairgrounds around the country, often competing side-by-side in fairgrounds; now there are four left. One is in a steam museum in Derbyshire, another is the hobby/toy of a Cornish builder, and a third is owned by a 54-year-old agricultural engineer who "has done everything in motorcycles except ridden a wall of death". That wall's old owner, Graham Cripsey, of the Cripsey fairground family, is coming down from Skegness to teach him how to ride it.

8    Only Ken Fox and his band, together with pet dog Freebie, two ferrets and two cockatiels, tour in the traditional way, squelching out of their winter quarters from behind the Cambridgeshire hedgerows just before Easter and heading in convoy for the first of the 6,000 miles they will complete by the end of October. Ken is lucky that Julie can drive one of the trucks, change the 2 ft-high tyres, make sure Alex does his school lessons on his laptop, cook, make sandwiches and dish out the £2 tickets. She, too, loves the travelling life. "When you think I used to be a dental nurse," she says, her eyes misting a little.

9    She also helped her husband build his wall of death. "My old wall was wearing out," he says, "so I bought a 200 ft section of very long,

very straight, Oregon pine that cost £70,000 (Oregon pine, one of the tallest trees in the world, is used for all walls of death because of the straightness of its grain and the lack of knot in its timber). I got the planks cut in a milling yard. I went to a boatyard where they built submarines. The place was so big we could have built 50 walls of death."

10    The motorbikes used for shows are Indian Scouts made in the 1920s by the Hendee Motorcycle Company of Springfield, Massachusetts, deliberately engineered for easy balance with all the controls on the left, so Chicago cops could use their right hands for drawing their revolvers and shooting at Al Capone-style gangsters. This means the bikes are perfect for tricks. Take your hand off the throttle of a modern motorbike and its slips back to idling mode, thus losing the power that keeps the bike on the wall. Take your hand off the throttle of an Indian Scout, and the revs stay as they are—which means that you can zoom round and round the wall of death, arms in the air, to your heart's content.

11    The first wall of death is said by Graham Cripsey to have come to Britain from America in 1928 with others close on its heels. His grandfather, Walter, and father, Roy, trained lions to ride in the sidecars, as did the famous George "Tornado" Smith at Southend's Kursaal fairground. The Cripseys also developed a technique of being towed round behind the Indian Scouts on roller skates. "If you were competing side by side in a fairground, you always had to have one stunt better than the other," explains Graham. Smith also kept a skeleton in a sidecar which, with a flick on a control, would suddenly sit bolt upright. And Ricky Abrey, 61, who rode with him as "The Black Baron", says Tornado perfected a ride where three riders would cut off their engines at the top of the wall and instantly re-start them again, causing the audience to gasp as 2 ft-long flashes of flame escaped the exhaust pipes.

12    Fun, then, for all the family. "People still love the wall of death," says Ken Fox emphatically. "People like what we put on and get good value for it. If they see it once, they always want to see it again. The problem is finding the people to work on it. There are a lot of soft men around."

13    "Wall of death" is, thankfully, a bit of a misnomer, for there have been no fatal accidents on British walls, though whether that's due to good luck or fear-induced careful preparation is difficult to tell. "I've been

knocked off by other riders, the engine's stalled, I've had punctures and I've hit a safety cable," says Ken Fox, pointing at his scars. "Everyone gets falls at some time but we try to be spot-on in our preparations. Before every show we spend a complete day trying to get the machines working perfectly."

14    Luke Fox suffered his first bad fall last year, flicking a safety-cable bolt on one of his "dips" as he zig-zagged his bike up and down. He fell 20 ft, got up and started again, even though he'd severely torn his knee. In a sense, he's got his own good-luck charm. His Indian bike was originally ridden by no less a daredevil than Tornado Smith himself. Luke has also inherited his father's total dedication to the trade and the Fox family wall looks set to last into the immediate future. Indeed, he and Kerri are now a partnership, sharing the long-haul driving and other things, while young Alex, the ferret-fancier, is raring for his first go at the wall.

15    Even Neil Calladine, the spieler, has shed his accountant duties and can indulge his lifelong passion for fairgrounds, though he needs to talk almost non-stop from 2 pm to 10 pm each show day and consumes mountains of throat sweets. "I make sure I go back and see the missus once a month," he says, "and of course I'm there all winter. I suppose I'm one of those fortunate people whose hobby has become his life. I love the freedom of travel, no nine-to-five, just us and the open road."

16    In that he's just like Kerri Cameron, bless her daredevil heart.

Adapted from an article
by John Dodd

[END OF PASSAGE]

[BLANK PAGE]

FOR OFFICIAL USE

**G**

Total
Mark

## 0860/404

NATIONAL
QUALIFICATIONS
2007

TUESDAY, 1 MAY
1.00 PM – 1.50 PM

**ENGLISH
STANDARD GRADE**
General Level
Reading
Questions

**Fill in these boxes and read what is printed below.**

Full name of centre

Town

Forename(s)

Surname

Date of birth
Day  Month  Year      Scottish candidate number      Number of seat

**NB Before leaving the examination room you must give this booklet to the invigilator.
If you do not, you may lose all the marks for this paper.**

SCOTTISH
QUALIFICATIONS
AUTHORITY

SA 0860/404  6/75170

*Marks*

## QUESTIONS

**Write your answers in the spaces provided.**

**Look at Paragraphs 1 to 3.**

1.  **In your own words**, explain fully why Kerri Cameron was looking up job vacancies on the internet.

    _____    2  1  0

2.  What is surprising about Kerri's reaction to what her mother tells her about the wall of death?

    _____

    _____    2  1  0

3.  Why do you think Ken Fox was not interested in Kerri's school qualifications?

    _____

    _____    2  ■  0

**Look at Paragraphs 4 and 5.**

4.  How does the writer suggest Kerri's enthusiasm after her test on the bike:

    (*a*)    by word choice?

    _____    2  ■  0

    (*b*)    by sentence structure?

    _____    2  ■  0

5.  **Using your own words as far as possible**, describe **two** aspects of Kerri's performance which could be described as dangerous.

    _____

    _____    2  1  0

PAGE
TOTAL

*Marks*

**Look at Paragraph 6.**

6. **In your own words**, explain the job of the "spieler".

_____

2   1   0

7. ". . . shower coins into the ring . . ."

Give **two** reasons why "shower" is an effective word to use in this context.

_____

_____

2   1   0

8. Why do you think members of the audience are told that wall-of-death riders "can never get insurance"?

_____

2   ■   0

9. Explain fully what the expression "zipping up, down and all around" suggests about the riders' performance.

_____

_____

2   1   0

**Look at Paragraphs 7 to 9.**

10. How does the writer illustrate the decline in popularity of walls of death?

_____

2   1   0

**[Turn over**

PAGE
TOTAL

*Marks*

11. "Only Ken Fox and his band . . ." (Paragraph 8)

Write down **one** word from earlier in the passage which contains the same idea as "band".

|   |   |
|---|---|

2 ■ 0

12. Explain fully why you think the writer uses the word "squelching" in Paragraph 8.

_____

_____

2 1 0

13. Look again at the sentence which begins "Ken is lucky . . ." (Paragraph 8).

How does the structure of the **whole** sentence help to reinforce how busy Julie is between Easter and October?

_____

_____

2 1 0

14. Why is Oregon pine so suitable for walls of death?

_____

2 1 0

**Look at Paragraph 10.**

15. **Using your own words as far as possible**, explain why the Indian Scout bikes are "perfect for tricks."

_____

_____

2 1 0

PAGE
TOTAL

*Marks*

16. **Identify two techniques** used by the writer which help to involve the reader in his description of the Indian Scout motorbikes. **Quote evidence** from the paragraph to support your answers.

| Technique | Evidence |
|-----------|----------|
|           |          |
|           |          |

2 1 0

2 1 0

**Look at Paragraphs 11 and 12.**

17. Why might the nicknames "Tornado" and "The Black Baron" be suitable for wall-of-death riders?

Tornado

_____

The Black Baron

_____    2 1 0

**[Turn over**

PAGE
TOTAL

*Marks*

**18.** (*a*)    Write down **four** things the early wall-of-death riders included in their acts.

_____

_____

_____

_____

2 | 1 | 0

(*b*)    **In your own words**, give **two** reasons why such things were included in the acts.

_____

_____

2 | 1 | 0

**Look at Paragraphs 13 to 16.**

**19.**    ". . . is, thankfully, a bit of a misnomer, . . ." (Paragraph 13)

(*a*)    Tick (✓) the box beside the best definition of "misnomer".

| | |
|---|---|
| old-fashioned attraction | |
| risky venture | |
| successful show | |
| wrongly applied name | |

(*b*)    Write down evidence from the passage to support your answer to 19(*a*).

_____

2 | 1 | 0

**20.**    Why is the word "dips" (Paragraph 14) in inverted commas?

_____

2 | ■ | 0

PAGE
TOTAL

*Marks*

**21.** Give **three** pieces of evidence to support the writer's statement that "the Fox family wall looks set to last into the immediate future" (Paragraph 14).

_____

_____

_____  2  1  0

**22.** Show how the final paragraph is an effective conclusion to this article.

_____

_____  2  1  0

*[END OF QUESTION PAPER]*

PAGE
TOTAL

FOR OFFICIAL USE

| | |
|---|---|
| p2 | |
| p3 | |
| p4 | |
| p5 | |
| p6 | |
| p7 | |
| TOTAL MARK | |

FOR OFFICIAL USE

# STANDARD GRADE | FOUNDATION

# 2008
## READING

[BLANK PAGE]

F

# 0860/401

NATIONAL
QUALIFICATIONS
2008

TUESDAY, 6 MAY
10.35 AM – 11.25 AM

ENGLISH
STANDARD GRADE
Foundation Level
Reading
Text

Read carefully the passage overleaf.  It will help if you read it twice.  When you have done so, answer the questions.  Use the spaces provided in the Question/Answer booklet.

# Home for Christmas

1    Christmas Eve was not a good day to hitch-hike. Billy had been at the motorway services for nearly five hours without a sniff of a lift. No-one had even slowed down to take a look at him. And the weather was lousy. At one point, he'd had to shelter from the rain next to some bins behind the petrol station. He'd dozed off, and there was another hour gone.

2    Now it was getting dark, and a fog was coming in. Cars drove by him as if he wasn't there. So much for Christmas spirit! It wasn't as though Billy had a big, off-putting bag either. All he carried was a small rucksack, which used to belong to his mum. It contained all his worldly goods, such as they were, and would fit beneath his legs in the smallest car.

3    Maybe he should cross the six-lane road, and try to hitch back to London, where he'd come from that morning. People said that you could get a bed and something to eat more easily at Christmas. But no. With Billy's luck, he'd probably get run over crossing the motorway.

4    Billy began to cough. He'd had this cold on and off for two months. Other homeless people told him that your body got used to the life, when you'd been living on the streets long enough. Maybe. He'd been sleeping rough for a year now. That was long enough for him to decide that it wasn't the life for him.

5    The fog was getting thicker. It was colder, too. When it got really dark, he'd wander into the café, warm up a bit. Billy had enough money left for a cup of coffee. That was, presuming they'd serve him. He looked a mess.

6    The rain started up again. Billy shivered. His jacket was supposed to be "shower-proof", but it was wet through. Puddles were forming around his feet. Suddenly, he saw a lorry, coming towards him from the direction of the petrol station. The lorry didn't have its lights on and was driving really close to the kerb. Instead of holding his thumb out, Billy took a step back. He didn't want to get splashed by the foul, oily water that lay on the road.

7    Still, the lorry seemed to be driving straight at him. Billy decided to get out of its way. But as he was about to make his move, the lorry turned its lights on, full beam. He couldn't see a thing. He stood there, frozen to the spot, like a rabbit dazzled by a poacher's torch, waiting to be shot.

8    The lorry stopped. One of its wheels was on the kerb, only centimetres from Billy's right foot. The passenger door opened. A deep voice spoke.

9    "You after a lift?"

10    It all felt wrong. Billy knew that. But it was raining hard now, and he had been there all day. He went up to the door and opened it a little farther.

11    "How far are you going?" the deep voice asked.

12    Billy still couldn't see the driver, only hear his harsh voice.

13    "I'm going to Scotland. To Gretna."

14    "I'm going that way myself. Get in."

15    Billy hesitated. He had learnt to walk away from threatening situations. But the man's accent was Scottish, like his, and he could take him all the way home—or, at least, to the place he used to call home.

16    Billy got into the cabin. He slid his bag beneath his feet and pulled on the seatbelt before looking at the driver.

17    "Thanks for stopping," he said. "It's pretty horrible out there."

18    The man said nothing. His thick hands reached for the gear stick. He began to accelerate onto the M1, towards the grim, frozen north.

19    In the half light of the lorry cabin, Billy looked at the driver. The man was in his late thirties, forty at most. He had short, dark hair. His eyes were set so deeply beneath his heavy eyebrows that Billy could barely make them out. His face was scarred. He was heavy set and wore a lumberjack shirt over shapeless jeans.

20    Billy hadn't done a lot of hitching, but he knew that there was an etiquette. The hitcher had to make conversation. It was your duty to entertain the driver, even if he didn't have a lot to say for himself. The driver had to concentrate on the driving, after all.

21    "I'm Billy," he said to the man, in his friendliest voice, "Billy Gates."

22    For a moment, he thought that the driver wasn't going to reply.

23    "Hank."

24    "Bad day to have to work, Christmas Eve."

25    Again, Hank didn't answer. Instead, he speeded up, until they were doing fifty. The fog was getting thicker and it felt too fast. Still, it wasn't Billy's place to say their speed was dangerous.

26    The silence was almost as threatening as the speed they were doing. There was a radio. Billy wondered whether he should suggest switching it on.

27    "Should I . . . ?"

28    Hank interrupted before Billy had formed the sentence.

29    "I don't like music."

30    The way he said it made Billy want to jump out of the cab, even though their speed was up to fifty-five and there was nothing but filthy fog outside. Instead, he began to say the first things that came into his mind.

31    "Do you know how many cars went by before you picked me up?"

32    Hank remained silent.

33    "A thousand at least."

34    Now that he'd starting talking, he couldn't stop.

35    "I think this time of year is a pain, really," Billy said. "You know what I mean? Everyone's expected to have a good time, so when you're not, somehow it seems a hundred times worse."

36    "Aye," said Hank. "I know that all right."

37    He began to drive even faster.

Adapted from a short story

*[END OF PASSAGE]*

[BLANK PAGE]

FOR OFFICIAL USE

F

Total
Mark

# 0860/402

NATIONAL
QUALIFICATIONS
2008

TUESDAY, 6 MAY
10.35 AM – 11.25 AM

ENGLISH
STANDARD GRADE
Foundation Level
Reading
Questions

**Fill in these boxes and read what is printed below.**

Full name of centre

Town

Forename(s)

Surname

Date of birth
Day  Month  Year

Scottish candidate number

Number of seat

**NB  Before leaving the examination room you must give this booklet to the invigilator. If you do not, you may lose all the marks for this paper.**

*Marks*

## QUESTIONS

**Write your answers in the spaces provided.**

**Look at Paragraphs 1 and 2.**

1. **When** and **where** does the story begin?

_____

_____    | 2 | 1 | 0 |

2. ". . . not a good day to hitch-hike."  (Paragraph 1)

   Give **two** pieces of evidence from Paragraph 1 which show this is true.

   (i) _____

   (ii) _____    | 2 | 1 | 0 |

3. Billy's situation becomes worse as it grows late.

   **Write down two** things from Paragraph 2 which add to his difficulties.

   (i) _____

   (ii) _____    | 2 | 1 | 0 |

4. **Write down an expression** from Paragraph 2 which shows that drivers paid no attention to Billy.

   _____    | 2 | ■ | 0 |

5. Billy is carrying a rucksack.

   Why would this **not** be a problem for drivers?

   _____    | 2 | ■ | 0 |

PAGE
TOTAL

*Marks*

**6.** Give **two** reasons why the rucksack might be important to Billy.

_____

_____    2  1  0

**Look at Paragraphs 3 to 5.**

**7.** Billy thinks about crossing the road and returning to London.

 (*a*)   Why does he consider doing this?

_____

_____    2  1  0

 (*b*)   Why does he decide **not** to?

_____    2  ■  0

**8.** Billy is in bad physical shape.

 (*a*)   **Write down two ways** the writer shows us this.

_____    2  1  0

 (*b*)   **Why** is Billy in such bad shape?

_____    2  1  0

**9.** Give **two** reasons why Billy plans to go into the café later.

 (i) _____

 (ii) _____    2  1  0

**10. Write down an expression** which suggests he is a bit unsure about going into the café.

_____    2  ■  0

**[Turn over**

PAGE
TOTAL

*Marks*

**Look at Paragraphs 6 and 7.**

11. The weather is making Billy more and more miserable.

    **Write down three** things which show this.

    (i) _____

    (ii) _____

    (iii) _____   2 1 0

12. **Why** has the writer put inverted commas around the word "shower-proof"?

    _____   2 ■ 0

13. When Billy **first** sees the lorry (Paragraph 6), which **two** things make it dangerous?

    (i) _____

    (ii) _____   2 1 0

14. ". . . like a rabbit dazzled by a poacher's torch, waiting to be shot." (Paragraph 7)

    (a) What technique is the writer using in this expression? Tick (✓) the correct box.

    | rhyme | |
    |---|---|
    | metaphor | |
    | alliteration | |
    | simile | |

      2 ■ 0

    (b) What **two** things does this expression suggest about Billy?

    (i) _____

    (ii) _____   2 1 0

PAGE TOTAL

*Marks*

**Look at Paragraphs 8 to 18.**

15. **Before** Billy gets into the lorry, how does the writer make the driver seem mysterious and threatening?

_____

    2   1   0

16. "Billy hesitated." (Paragraph 15)

Give **two** reasons why he then decides to accept the lift after all.

(i) _____

(ii) _____

    2   1   0

17. ". . . —or, at least, to the place he used to call home." (Paragraph 15)

How do you think Billy feels about his home in Scotland?

_____

    2   ■   0

18. ". . . the grim, frozen north." (Paragraph 18)

**Explain** why this is a good description of Billy's destination.

_____

    2   1   0

**Look at Paragraphs 19 and 20.**

19. ". . . etiquette." (Paragraph 20)

Tick (✓) the box beside the best definition of "etiquette".

| | |
|---|---|
| a conversation | |
| a gadget | |
| a way of behaving correctly | |
| a solution to a problem | |

    2   ■   0

**[Turn over for Questions 20 to 22 on *Page six***

*Marks*

**Look at Paragraphs 21 to 37.**

**20.** Billy becomes more and more nervous.

**Write down three** things about Hank's behaviour which make Billy feel like this.

(i) _____

(ii) _____

(iii) _____    **2  1  0**

**21.** "Everyone's expected to have a good time . . ."  (Paragraph 35)

**Why** does this bother Billy?

_____

_____    **2  1  0**

**Think about the passage as a whole.**

**22.** Do you feel sorry for Billy?

Tick (✓) **one** box.

Yes  [    ]

No  [    ]

Give **two** reasons from the passage to support your answer.

(i) _____

_____

(ii) _____

_____    **2  1  0**

*[END OF QUESTION PAPER]*

PAGE TOTAL

FOR OFFICIAL USE

|        |     |
|--------|-----|
| p2     |     |
| p3     |     |
| p4     |     |
| p5     |     |
| p6     |     |
| TOTAL MARK |  |

FOR OFFICIAL USE

[BLANK PAGE]

# STANDARD GRADE | GENERAL

# 2008
## READING

[BLANK PAGE]

**G**

# 0860/403

NATIONAL
QUALIFICATIONS
2008

TUESDAY, 6 MAY
1.00 PM – 1.50 PM

ENGLISH
STANDARD GRADE
General Level
Reading
Text

Read carefully the passage overleaf. It will help if you read it twice. When you have done so, answer the questions. Use the spaces provided in the Question/Answer booklet.

# Saddle the white horses

Thurso prepares to host its first professional surf tour, confirming Scotland's status as a world–class surfing destination.

1   It was the stickers that gave it away. Turning left on the A9 at Latheron in Caithness, you were suddenly faced with a sign that looked as though it had been defaced by advertising executives from surfing companies. Like a cairn on a mountain path, the big green board declaring Thurso to be 23 miles away told travelling bands of surfers that they'd taken the right turn-off and were nearly at their destination. Slapping another sticker on the sign was like laying another stone on the pile.

2   Thurso is about to enter surfing's big league.

3   It's hard to reconcile the popular tropical imagery of surfing with the town, a raw, exposed kind of place that enjoys little escape from the worst excesses of the Scottish climate. The Caithness coastline is peppered with surfing spots, but the jewel in the crown and the target for dedicated wave riders lies within spitting distance of Thurso town centre at a reef break called Thurso East. In the right conditions, the swell there rears up over kelp-covered slabs into a fast-moving, barrelling monster of a wave considered world class by those in the know.

4   Now Thurso East is the focus of a huge professional surfing tour. The week-long Highland Open marks the first time a World Qualifying Series (WQS) surfing competition has been held in Scotland. It will also be the furthest north a WQS tour has ever travelled, anywhere in the world.

5   Professional competitive surfing has two tours: the WQS and the World Championship Tour (WCT). The WCT is the premier division, with the WQS being used as a platform for professionals to move up into the big time. Around 160 up-and-coming wave riders are expected to take part in the Thurso event. Prize money of $100,000 (£57,000) is up for grabs, along with vital tour points.

6   "Travelling and exploring new places is part of the whole surfing culture," says Bernhard Ritzer, the Highland Open event manager. "We've had so much feedback from surfers from Australia and Brazil who want to go. They see it as an adventure and as something new. We did a photo trip there last year with some of our team riders and they were impressed. They're excited about it—although it will still be a shock because I don't think they know how cold and harsh it can be."

7   "Thurso is one of the best waves in Europe, if not the world," he says. "Most people don't even know it, and it's just so good. It doesn't always have to be sunny, warm and tropical. It can also be cold, rough and hard.

8   "The idea is to have a contrast to the summer events in the tropical islands. We also have something in the north to show that this is part of surfing. Very often on the WQS tour the waves aren't that good, but here they are expecting big reef break waves and they like to surf those."

9   Surfers generally guard their local breaks jealously. It's considered essential to keep your mouth shut about your "secret spot", in case you find it overrun with visitors. So, economic benefits to Thurso aside, some local surfers were a little concerned about an event on this scale descending on their area. WQS representatives met with these surfers to address their concerns and feel that they've pretty much got everyone on board. WQS is also paying for improvements to the car parking area near the Thurso East break.

10   "We're concerned to get the locals involved," says Ritzer. "We want to keep them happy and don't want to look too commercial, coming in with a big event machine. We need them to help organise local stuff. You always have some individuals who will boycott everything, but we understand that most of them are positive."

11    Andy Bain probably knows the break at Thurso East better than anyone, although he'll be watching the competition from the shoreline. Bain, who runs Thurso Surf, has been surfing the reef there for 17 years and is eagerly anticipating the arrival of the Highland Open. He's aware of the concerns and the possible exposure of his home break, but doesn't anticipate a negative impact.

12    "From the surf school side of things it's good because it'll generate business for us," says Bain, 33. "As a local surfer, it's kind of like closure for me to have this competition. To say the world has now recognised Thurso as a top surfing destination makes me feel proud. A lot of people say it's going to get crowded and exposed, but with it being a cold destination I don't think it's going to be that bad."

13    For professional surfer Adam Robertson from Victoria, Australia, the trip to Thurso will be something of a journey into the unknown. "This will be the first time I've ever been to Scotland," says Robertson, who has competed on the WQS tour for the past three years. "We're all a bit worried about how cold it's going to be. Apart from that we're pretty excited because it's a place we've never been."

14    Robertson, 23, who has been surfing since he was four, criss-crosses the globe with his fellow WQS competitors in pursuit of the best waves and a place on the coveted WCT tour. He may as well be going to surf on the moon for all he knows about Thurso East, but that's part of the appeal.

15    "We follow the surf around all year and go to a lot of different places, but Scotland's somewhere probably none of us have been to," he says. "That for me was a big part of wanting to go, to see the place. As a professional surfer, you've got to live out of your bag a lot, travelling around with long stints away from home, but when you perform well in the event or get some really good waves, it makes it all worth it.

16    "I feel pretty good and I'm hoping to do well," he adds. "Everyone who does the tour is feeling good too, so it should be a great event. It'll be interesting to see what the waves are like."

17    Competitors will be scored by a team of eight international judges on the length of their ride, the difficulty of moves and how they connect it all together. Waves are scored on a one to ten scale, with ten a perfect ride, and the final scores are based on each surfer's two highest-scoring waves.

18    "These events raise the profile of locations, create investment in areas and hopefully provide opportunities for young surfers coming through to grow and compete at world-class levels," says Dave Reed, contest director for the WQS event. "It's a great way to say we've got some of the best waves in the world."

Adapted from a magazine article

[END OF PASSAGE]

[BLANK PAGE]

FOR OFFICIAL USE

| | | | | | |
|---|---|---|---|---|---|

**G**

Total
Mark

# 0860/404

NATIONAL
QUALIFICATIONS
2008

TUESDAY, 6 MAY
1.00 PM – 1.50 PM

ENGLISH
STANDARD GRADE
General Level
Reading
Questions

**Fill in these boxes and read what is printed below.**

Full name of centre

Town

Forename(s)

Surname

Date of birth
Day  Month  Year

Scottish candidate number

Number of seat

**NB  Before leaving the examination room you must give this booklet to the invigilator.
If you do not, you may lose all the marks for this paper.**

SA 0860/404  6/66870

*Marks*

## QUESTIONS

**Write your answers in the spaces provided.**

**Look at Paragraphs 1 to 3.**

1. (*a*) What had been added to the road sign in Caithness?

   _____   2 ■ 0

   (*b*) Write down **two** things the surfers would know when they saw this road sign.

   _____

   _____   2 1 0

2. "Thurso is about to enter surfing's big league." (Paragraph 2)

   How does the writer make this statement stand out?

   _____   2 ■ 0

3. Thurso is different from the popular image of a surfing location.

   (*a*) **In your own words**, describe the popular image of a surfing location.

   _____   2 ■ 0

   (*b*) **Write down an expression** showing how Thurso is different.

   _____   2 ■ 0

4. What do the words "jewel in the crown" (Paragraph 3) suggest about Thurso East?

   _____   2 ■ 0

5. ". . . a fast-moving, barrelling monster . . ." (Paragraph 3)

   Explain fully why this is an effective description of the wave.

   _____

   _____   2 1 0

PAGE
TOTAL

*Marks*

**Look at Paragraphs 4 and 5.**

6. In which **two** ways is the Highland Open different from other WQS surfing competitions?

    (i) _____

    (ii) _____   2  1  0

7. **In your own words**, explain the difference between the two professional surfing tours.

    WCT _____

    WQS _____   2  1  0

8. Which **two** benefits will the winner of the competition gain?

    (i) _____

    (ii) _____   2  1  0

**Look at Paragraphs 6 to 8.**

9. Give **three** reasons why, according to Bernhard Ritzer, surfers will want to visit Thurso.

    (i) _____

    (ii) _____

    (iii) _____   2  1  0

10. According to Ritzer, what will surprise the surfers?

    _____   2  ■  0

**[Turn over**

*Marks*

**11.** Thurso can offer something which many other surfing locations cannot.

What is this?

_____    2 ■ 0

**Look at Paragraphs 9 and 10.**

**12.** "Surfers generally guard their local breaks . . . " (Paragraph 9)

**In your own words**, explain why surfers do this.

_____    2 1 0

**13.** What **style** of language is used in the expression "keep your mouth shut" (Paragraph 9)?

_____    2 ■ 0

**14.** Which **two key** things have WQS representatives done to gain support?

(i) _____

(ii) _____    2 1 0

**15.** The WQS representatives feel that "they've pretty much got everyone on board." (Paragraph 9)

**Write down an expression** from Paragraph 10 which continues this idea.

_____    2 ■ 0

**16. Write down a single word** from this section meaning "refuse to support or take part".

_____

2 ■ 0

*Marks*

**Look at Paragraphs 11 to 18.**

**17.** (*a*)  How does local surfer Andy Bain feel about the competition?

Tick (✓) the best answer.

| | |
|---|---|
| very negative and angry | |
| quite pleased but worried | |
| excited and not really anxious | |

2 ■ 0

(*b*)  **Write down an expression** to support your chosen answer.

_____

2 ■ 0

**18.**  "He may as well be going to surf on the moon . . . " (Paragraph 14)

What does this comparison suggest about Thurso?

_____

2 ■ 0

**19.**  In Paragraph 15, Australian Adam Robertson describes his life as a professional surfer.

**In your own words**, sum up the **negative** and **positive** aspects of his life.

(*a*)  **negative:** _____

_____

2 1 0

(*b*)  **positive:** _____

_____

2 1 0

**20.**  What **three** elements of the surfers' performance are judged?

(i) _____

(ii) _____

(iii) _____

2 1 0

**[Turn over**

PAGE
TOTAL

*Marks*

**Think about the passage as a whole.**

21.   (i)  What do you think is the main purpose of this passage?

Tick (✓) **one** box.

| | |
|---|---|
| to tell the reader some amusing stories about surfing | |
| to inform the reader about a surfing competition in Scotland | |
| to argue against holding a surfing competition in Scotland | |

(ii)  Give a reason to support your answer.

_____

_____    2   1   0

*[END OF QUESTION PAPER]*

PAGE
TOTAL

FOR OFFICIAL USE

|  |  |
|---|---|
| p2 | ☐ |
| p3 | ☐ |
| p4 | ☐ |
| p5 | ☐ |
| p6 | ☐ |
| TOTAL MARK | ☐ |

[BLANK PAGE]

# STANDARD GRADE | FOUNDATION

## 2009
### READING

[BLANK PAGE]

F

# 0860/401

NATIONAL
QUALIFICATIONS
2009

FRIDAY, 8 MAY
10.35 AM – 11.25 AM

ENGLISH
STANDARD GRADE
Foundation Level
Reading
Text

Read carefully the passage overleaf.  It will help if you read it twice.  When you have done so, answer the questions.  Use the spaces provided in the Question/Answer booklet.

*In the following passage, Tom, a boy who has just arrived in Australia, is taken on a trip by his new friends, Sam and Greg.*

1    They camped much later that afternoon on top of a low cliff above the river.  The river was lined with trees.  They reminded Tom of children's drawings with their square-shaped trunks and stubby little branches.

2    The river glided over polished white boulders.  There were lily pads a metre wide with huge purple flowers at their centre.  The nearest pads were about thirty metres away.  Bright green ferns grew amongst the cracks in the rocky sides.

3    Tom looked round to see what the others were doing then scrambled down to the river's edge.  There was a wide sandy beach on the opposite bank.  Tom studied it.  It wouldn't take any time to swim there and back and he wanted a swim very badly.  He was sweat-stained and tired.  There was sand in his hair, under his fingernails and inside his shorts.

4    He slipped off his shoes and stood ankle deep in the water.  He closed his eyes and let the sensation engulf him.  The water felt like silk.  He took a deep breath and slowly let it out.  The stress of the day began to disappear.  He could stay here for ever, he decided.  A bird shrilled from a nearby bush.  He waded further out.

5    "Hey!" Sam's shout interrupted his sense of well-being.  "Tom!  Get back!  What the heck you doing!"  He came scrambling down the rocks in a flurry of arms and legs.  He grabbed Tom's arm and dragged him away.

6    "You want to see your mother again?" he hissed, putting his face into Tom's.  "You want to get me into big trouble?"  He scowled at Tom.  "You think you know better than me?"

7    "Hey look!  I'm sorry . . ." began Tom.

8    "Me too," Sam snapped.  Then he shook his head.  "It's my fault.  I forgot to tell you about crocodiles.  Saltwater crocodiles.  The scariest in the world.  I'm a stupid man."

9    It was Tom's turn to reassure.  "Don't worry," he said.  "I had a really good look before I came down.  There was nothing there.  I promise you."

10    Sam cleared his throat and spat on to the sand.  "See those lily pads?" he pointed, grabbing Tom's arm.  "The crocs hide under there and watch.  They don't miss a trick.  They can stay there all day, waiting.  Then an animal like you comes along and thinks everything is safe."  He clapped his hands together.  "Big mistake!"

11    He shook his finger at Tom.  "Want to know how bad it is?" he said.  "Most families round here have someone taken by a croc every year."

12    Tom's mouth dropped.

13    Sam shrugged.  "That's how it goes," he said.  "Think you can run fast?" he asked and without waiting for Tom's reply added, "No man alive can outrun a crocodile.  They can do twenty miles an hour over fifty metres."  He grinned suddenly at Tom.  "You get chased by a six-metre-long saltwater with its jaws open, it's time to say goodbye, my friend.  Ain't nothing that can help you then."

14    "Hey!  You guys!" came Greg's voice from above.  "Come and give us a hand!  I'm not making camp on my own!"

15    They hurried back to the vehicle.  Greg had already unpacked a small mound of stores.  They all set to and very quickly had put up the tent, two camp beds and got the food organised.

16    "Doesn't Sam have a bed?"  Tom asked, looking round inside the tent.

17    Sam shook his head.  "Always sleep on the ground."

18    "Keeps the snakes from coming inside!" Greg laughed.

19    Later, Tom went off with Sam to collect wood for the camp fire.  There was plenty lying around and all of it tinder dry.  Tom worked steadily picking up branches and dragging them into a pile.  He stopped under a tree and took a breather.  He looked up and was puzzled to see a number of triangular-shaped leaves hanging down from a branch.

20    Tom stared at them.  He had never seen leaves this shape or size before.  Then he noticed that they weren't just a single leaf but several, all joined together.  Intrigued, he picked up a long thin stick and tapped the nearest one.

21    Seconds later the whole branch was boiling over with enraged ants.  But ants of a kind he had never seen before.  Bright green ants in their thousands swarmed over every inch of the bark.  Some fell on to his arm and he yelled in surprise.  It felt as if a dozen red-hot injection needles had suddenly been thrust through his skin.  He ran, slapping at them.  Sam thought it a great joke and picked a whole lot more from Tom's hair.

22    "They're bad, those things," Greg remarked, when they got back to camp.  "Probably kill you if enough got hold of you.  Bit stupid of you annoying 'em.  This isn't a park in London, you know."

23    Tom said nothing.  Greg as usual was right.  Then, while Sam went off to check the vehicle, he helped Greg build the fire.  Tom watched Greg dig a shallow hole.  "Aren't we going to have a bonfire?" Tom asked.

24    Greg stared at him.  "Take a look around," he advised.  "If this place catches fire we're all dead men.  Ever seen a bush fire before?"

25    Tom thought of the muddy paths that criss-crossed the woods back home.  He shook his head.  How could he?

26    "You get a wall of fire metres high in a couple of minutes," Greg told him.  "Goes across the ground faster than you can drive.  This way, we keep the sparks down.  In the morning, you just fill it back in with earth.  Simple and safe."

27    Greg opened a packet of firelighters and pulled one out.  Tom saw they were the same ones that his grandmother used back home.  He was amused.  "Why aren't you rubbing sticks together or something?" he joked.

28    Greg looked up at him, puzzled.  "Don't be daft," he said.  "What do you think matches are for?"

Adapted from the novel "Crocodile River" by Geoffrey Malone

*[END OF PASSAGE]*

[BLANK PAGE]

FOR OFFICIAL USE

F

Total
Mark

# 0860/402

NATIONAL
QUALIFICATIONS
2009

FRIDAY, 8 MAY
10.35 AM – 11.25 AM

ENGLISH
STANDARD GRADE
Foundation Level
Reading
Questions

**Fill in these boxes and read what is printed below.**

Full name of centre

Town

Forename(s)

Surname

Date of birth
Day  Month  Year

Scottish candidate number

Number of seat

**NB  Before leaving the examination room you must give this booklet to the invigilator.
If you do not, you may lose all the marks for this paper.**

*Marks*

## QUESTIONS

**Write your answers in the spaces provided.**

**Look at Paragraphs 1 and 2.**

1. What kind of trip were Tom and his friends on?

   _____    2 ■ 0

2. The river was moving smoothly. Write down **one** word from Paragraph 2 which shows this.

   _____    2 ■ 0

3. In the countryside around Tom, things were **large** and **colourful**. Write down **one** example of something large and **one** example of something colourful around Tom.

   large: _____

   colourful: _____    2 1 0

**Look at Paragraphs 3 to 6.**

4. Give **three** reasons why Tom "wanted a swim very badly". (Paragraph 3)

   (i) _____

   (ii) _____

   (iii) _____    2 1 0

PAGE
TOTAL

*Marks*

**5.** "The water felt like silk." (Paragraph 4)

   (*a*)   What technique is the writer using in this expression?  Tick (✓) the correct box.

| | |
|---|---|
| metaphor | |
| simile | |
| alliteration | |
| contrast | |

2  ■  0

   (*b*)   What does this expression suggest about how the water felt?

   _____

2  ■  0

**6.** Why did Tom feel he "could stay here for ever"?  (Paragraph 4)

   _____

2  ■  0

**7.** What stopped Tom from enjoying the water?

   _____

2  1  0

**8.** Sam was clearly angry with Tom.

   Write down **one thing he did to Tom** and **one thing he said** which clearly showed he was angry.

   (i) _____

   (ii) _____

2  1  0

**[Turn over**

PAGE
TOTAL

*Marks*

**Look at Paragraphs 7 to 9.**

9. Why did Sam call himself "a stupid man"?  (Paragraph 8)

_____     2  1  0

10. Explain fully why Tom thought the water was safe.

_____

_____     2  1  0

**Look at Paragraphs 10 to 13.**

11. In Paragraph 10, Sam explained that crocodiles are good hunters.
    Write down **two** things from Paragraph 10 which show they are good hunters.

    (i) _____

    (ii) _____     2  1  0

12. Why did Tom's mouth drop?  (Paragraph 12)

_____     2  ■  0

13. Write down **two** pieces of evidence from Paragraph 13 which show how fast a crocodile can move.

    (i) _____

    (ii) _____     2  1  0

**Look at Paragraphs 15 to 17.**

14. Tom thinks something is missing from the tent.  **What** does he think is missing and **why** is it not needed?

_____

_____     2  1  0

PAGE
TOTAL

*Marks*

**Look at Paragraphs 19 and 20.**

**15.** Tom was "intrigued" by the strange leaves.  (Paragraph 20)

What does this mean he wanted to do?  Tick (✓) the best answer.

| | |
|---|---|
| eat them | |
| count them | |
| destroy them | |
| learn about them | |

2 ■ 0

**Look at Paragraph 21.**

**16.** Explain why "boiling over" is a good way to describe the ants.

_____

_____

2 ■ 0

**17.** When the ants landed on Tom, it felt like "a dozen red-hot injection needles".
Give **two** reasons why it felt like this.

(i) _____

(ii) _____

2 1 0

**18.** How do we know that Sam was not very worried about the ant attack?

_____

2 ■ 0

**Look at Paragraphs 22 to 27.**

**19.** What did Greg mean when he said "This isn't a park in London"?  (Paragraph 22)

_____

2 ■ 0

**[Turn over for Questions 20 to 24 on *Page six***

PAGE
TOTAL

Marks

**20.** What did Greg do to make sure their fire was safe?

_____   2 ■ 0

**21.** Explain fully why the boys had to be careful about the fire.

_____

_____   2 1 0

**22.** "Simple and safe."  (Paragraph 26)

What makes this expression stand out?

_____   2 ■ 0

**23.** Why was Tom "amused" when he saw the firelighters?  (Paragraph 27)

_____

_____   2 1 0

**Think about the passage as a whole.**

**24.** Tick (✓) the word which you feel best sums up Tom's experience of camping.

| | |
|---|---|
| terrifying | |
| exciting | |
| embarrassing | |

Give **two** pieces of evidence from the passage to support your answer.

(i) _____

(ii) _____   2 1 0

*[END OF QUESTION PAPER]*

PAGE
TOTAL

FOR OFFICIAL USE

| | |
|---|---|
| p2 | |
| p3 | |
| p4 | |
| p5 | |
| p6 | |
| TOTAL MARK | |

[BLANK PAGE]

[BLANK PAGE]

G

**0860/403**

NATIONAL
QUALIFICATIONS
2009

FRIDAY, 8 MAY
1.00 PM – 1.50 PM

# ENGLISH
## STANDARD GRADE
General Level
Reading
Text

Read carefully the passage overleaf. It will help if you read it twice. When you have done so, answer the questions. Use the spaces provided in the Question/Answer booklet.

*In the following passage, Alice, the main character, is spending the summer working in France.*

1    Alice notices a fly on the underside of her arm.

2    Insects are an occupational hazard at a dig, and for some reason there are more flies higher up the mountain where she is working than at the main excavation site lower down.

3    Her concentration broken, Alice stands up and stretches.  She unscrews the top of her water bottle.  It's warm, but she's too thirsty to care and drinks it down in great gulps.  Below, the heat haze shimmers above the dented tarmac of the road.  Above her, the sky is an endless blue.

4    It's her first time in the Pyrenees, although she feels very much at home.  In the main camp on the lower slopes, Alice can see her colleagues standing under the big canvas awning.  She's surprised they've stopped already.  It's early in the day to be taking a break, but then the whole team is a bit demoralised.  It's hard work:  the digging, scraping, cataloguing, recording, and so far they've turned up little to justify their efforts.  They've come across only a few fragments of early medieval pots and bowls, and a couple of arrowheads.

5    Alice is tempted to go down and join her colleagues.  Her calves are already aching from squatting.  The muscles in her shoulders are tense.  But she knows that if she stops now, she'll lose her momentum.

6    Hopefully, her luck's about to change.  Earlier, she'd noticed something glinting beneath a large boulder, propped against the side of the mountain, almost as if it had been placed there by a giant hand.  Although she can't make out what the object is, even how big it is, she's been digging all morning and she doesn't think it will be much longer before she can reach it.

7    She knows she should fetch someone.  Alice is not a trained archaeologist, just a volunteer.  But it's her last day on site and she wants to prove herself.  If she goes back down to the main camp now and admits she's on to something, everybody will want to be involved, and it will no longer be her discovery.

8    In the days and weeks to come, Alice will look back to this moment.  She will wonder at how different things might have been had she made the choice to go and not to stay.  If she had played by the rules.

9    She drains the last drop of water from the bottle and tosses it into her rucksack.  For the next hour or so, as the sun climbs higher in the sky and the temperature rises, Alice carries on working.  The only sounds are the scrape of metal on rock, the whine of insects and the occasional buzz of a light aircraft in the distance.

10    Alice kneels down on the ground and leans her cheek and shoulder against the rock for support.  Then, with a flutter of excitement, she pushes her fingers deep into the dark earth.  Straight away, she knows she's got something worth finding.  It is smooth to the touch, metal not stone.  Grasping it firmly and telling herself not to expect too much, slowly, slowly she eases the object out into the light.

11    The rich, cloying smell of wet soil fills her nose and throat, although she barely notices.  She is already lost in the past, captivated by the piece of history she cradles in the palms of her hands.  It is a heavy, round buckle, speckled black and green with age and from its long burial.

12    Alice is so absorbed that she doesn't notice the boulder shifting on its base. Then something makes her look up. For a split second, the world seems to hang suspended, out of space, out of time. She is mesmerised by the ancient slab of stone as it sways and tilts, and then gracefully begins to fall towards her. At the very last moment, the light fractures. The spell is broken. Alice throws herself out of the way, half tumbling, half slithering sideways, just in time to avoid being crushed. The boulder hits the ground with a dull thud, sending up a cloud of pale brown dust, then rolls over and over, as if in slow motion, until it comes to rest further down the mountain.

13    Alice clutches desperately at the bushes and scrub to stop herself slipping any further. For a moment she lies sprawled in the dirt, dizzy and disorientated. As it sinks in how very close she came to being crushed, she turns cold. Takes a deep breath. Waits for the world to stop spinning.

14    Gradually, the pounding in her head dies away. The sickness in her stomach settles and everything starts to return to normal, enough for her to sit up and take stock. Her knees are grazed and streaked with blood and she's knocked her wrist where she landed awkwardly, still clutching the buckle in her hand to protect it, but basically she's escaped with no more than a few cuts and bruises.

15    She gets to her feet and dusts herself down. She raises her hand, is about to call out to attract someone's attention when she notices that there's a narrow opening visible in the side of the mountain where the boulder had been standing. Like a doorway cut into the rock.

16    She hesitates. Alice knows she should get somebody to come with her. It is stupid, possibly even dangerous, to go in on her own without any sort of back-up. She knows all the things that can go wrong. But something is drawing her in. It feels personal. It's her discovery.

17    She climbs back up. There is a dip in the ground at the mouth of the cave, where the stone had stood guard. The damp earth is alive with the frantic writhing of worms and beetles exposed suddenly to the light and heat after so long. Her cap lies on the ground where it fell. Her trowel is there too, just where she left it.

18    Alice peers into the darkness. The opening is no more than five feet high and about three feet wide and the edges are irregular and rough. It seems to be natural rather than man-made.

19    Slowly, her eyes become accustomed to the gloom. Velvet black gives way to charcoal grey and she sees that she is looking into a long, narrow tunnel.

20    Squeezing the buckle tightly in her hand, she takes a deep breath and steps forward into the passageway. Straight away, the smell of long-hidden, underground air surrounds her, filling her mouth and throat and lungs. It's cool and damp, not the dry, poisonous gases of a sealed cave she's been warned about, so she guesses there must be some source of fresh air.

21    Feeling nervous and slightly guilty, Alice wraps the buckle in a handkerchief and pushes it into her pocket, then cautiously steps forward.

22    As she moves further in, she feels the chill air curl around her bare legs and arms like a cat. She is walking downhill. She can feel the ground sloping away beneath her feet, uneven and gritty. The scrunch of the stones and gravel is loud in the confined, hushed space. She is aware of the daylight getting fainter and fainter at her back, the further and deeper she goes.

23    Abruptly, she does not want to go on.

Adapted from the novel "Labyrinth" by Kate Mosse

*[END OF PASSAGE]*

[BLANK PAGE]

FOR OFFICIAL USE

| | | | | | |
|---|---|---|---|---|---|
| | | | | | |

Total Mark

**G**

# 0860/404

NATIONAL
QUALIFICATIONS
2009

FRIDAY, 8 MAY
1.00 PM – 1.50 PM

**ENGLISH
STANDARD GRADE**
General Level
Reading
Questions

---

**Fill in these boxes and read what is printed below.**

Full name of centre

Town

Forename(s)

Surname

Date of birth
Day Month Year    Scottish candidate number    Number of seat

**NB  Before leaving the examination room you must give this booklet to the invigilator.
If you do not, you may lose all the marks for this paper.**

Marks

## QUESTIONS

**Write your answers in the spaces provided.**

**Look at Paragraphs 1 and 2.**

1.  What activity is Alice involved in?

    _____    2 ■ 0

2.  "Insects are an occupational hazard . . . " (Paragraph 2)

    Explain **in your own words** what this means.

    _____

    _____    2 1 0

**Look at Paragraphs 3 to 5.**

3.  Write down **three** things the writer tells us in Paragraph 3 which show that it is a hot day.

    (i) _____

    (ii) _____

    (iii) _____    2 1 0

4.  How does the writer emphasise that "It's hard work"? (Paragraph 4)

    (a)  by sentence structure

        _____    2 ■ 0

    (b)  by word choice

        _____    2 ■ 0

5.  Write down an expression from the passage which suggests the hard work has not been worth it so far.

    _____    2 ■ 0

*Marks*

**6.** "Alice is tempted to go down and join her colleagues." (Paragraph 5)

Give **two** reasons why she is tempted to do this.

(i) _____

(ii) _____    2  1  0

**Look at Paragraph 7.**

**7.** Tick (✓) the appropriate box to show whether the following statements about Alice are True, False or Cannot Tell from the passage.

|  | True | False | Cannot Tell |  |
|---|---|---|---|---|
| She wants to show that she can do the job herself. |  |  |  | 2 ■ 0 |
| She does not like her colleagues. |  |  |  | 2 ■ 0 |
| She wants to share her discovery. |  |  |  | 2 ■ 0 |

**Look at Paragraph 10.**

**8.** In Paragraph 10, the writer shows Alice's **feelings** and **thoughts** as she pushes her hand into the soil.

(*a*) **Write down one** expression which shows her **feelings** at this point.

_____    2 ■ 0

(*b*) **Write down one** expression which shows her **thoughts** at this point.

_____    2 ■ 0

**9.** Why does the writer repeat the word "slowly" in Paragraph 10?

_____    2 ■ 0

**[Turn over**

PAGE TOTAL

*Marks*

**Look at Paragraphs 11 and 12.**

10. Alice is "captivated" by the buckle she has found.  (Paragraph 11)

    Write down **one** other word from the next paragraph (Paragraph 12) which **also** shows how interested she is in the buckle.

    ```
    ┌──────────────────────────────────┐
    │                                  │
    │                                  │
    └──────────────────────────────────┘
    ```

    2 ■ 0

11. Give **two** reasons why Alice does not move out of the way of the boulder until the last moment.

    (i) _____

    (ii) _____

    2 1 0

12. Explain carefully what is surprising about the word "gracefully" in Paragraph 12.

    _____

    2 1 0

**Look at Paragraphs 13 to 16.**

13. " . . . dirt, dizzy and disorientated."  (Paragraph 13)

    Identify the **technique** used here.

    _____

    2 ■ 0

14. **In your own words**, explain why Alice "turns cold".  (Paragraph 13)

    _____

    _____

    2 1 0

15. Why do you think Alice does **not** "call out to attract someone's attention"? (Paragraph 15)

    _____

    _____

    2 1 0

PAGE TOTAL

*Marks*

**Look at Paragraphs 17 to 19.**

**16.** "... the stone had stood guard."  (Paragraph 17)

Give **two** reasons why this expression is appropriate.

(i) _____

(ii) _____   2 1 0


**17.** "Slowly, her eyes become accustomed to the gloom."  (Paragraph 19)

Explain how the writer develops this idea in the next sentence.

_____

_____   2 1 0


**Look at Paragraph 21 to the end of the passage.**

**18.** As Alice steps into the tunnel, she experiences **two** feelings.  **In your own words**, explain what these **two** feelings are.

(i) _____

(ii) _____   2 1 0


**19.** "Abruptly, she does not want to go on."  (Paragraph 23)

Give **two** reasons why this is an effective ending to the passage.

(i) _____

(ii) _____   2 1 0


**[Turn over**

PAGE
TOTAL

*Marks*

**Think about the passage as a whole.**

20. The writer has written this story in the present tense.

    Why do you think the writer has done this?

    _____    2 ■ 0

21. What do you think will happen next in the story?

    Tick (✓) the answer which you think is most likely.

    | | |
    |---|---|
    | Alice will return to her colleagues. | |
    | Alice will go further into the cave and make an exciting discovery. | |
    | Alice will be trapped in the cave. | |

    Give **two** pieces of evidence from the passage to support your answer.

    (i) _____

    (ii) _____    2 1 0

[END OF QUESTION PAPER]

PAGE
TOTAL

FOR OFFICIAL USE

p2  ☐

p3  ☐

p4  ☐

p5  ☐

p6  ☐

TOTAL
MARK  ☐

FOR OFFICIAL USE

[BLANK PAGE]

STANDARD GRADE | FOUNDATION | GENERAL | CREDIT

# 2006
## WRITING

[BLANK PAGE]

**F
G
C**

## 0860/407

NATIONAL
QUALIFICATIONS
2006

WEDNESDAY, 3 MAY
9.00 AM – 10.15 AM

ENGLISH
STANDARD GRADE
Foundation, General
and Credit Levels
Writing

### Read This First

1  Inside this booklet, there are photographs and words.
   Use them to help you when you are thinking about what to write.
   Look at all the material and think about all the possibilities.

2  There are 21 assignments altogether for you to choose from.

3  Decide which assignment you are going to attempt.
   Choose only **one** and write its number in the margin of your answer book.

4  Pay close attention to what you are asked to write.
   **Plan** what you are going to write.
   Read and check your work before you hand it in.
   Any changes to your work should be made clearly.

SCOTTISH
QUALIFICATIONS
AUTHORITY

    ©

FIRST     **Look at the picture opposite.**
          **It shows a couple parting.**

NEXT      Think how you might feel about leaving someone you care for.

> WHAT YOU HAVE TO WRITE

1. **Write about** a time when you were separated from someone you cared about.

   You should concentrate on your **thoughts and feelings**.

   **OR**

2. **Write a short story** using the title:

   Never Forgotten.

   **OR**

3. We should be less afraid to speak openly about our feelings.
   **Discuss.**

   **OR**

4. **Write in any way you choose** using the picture opposite as your inspiration.

**[Turn over**

FIRST        **Look at the picture opposite.**
             **It shows a lightning strike.**


NEXT         Think about the power of storms.


WHAT YOU HAVE TO WRITE


5.  **Describe** both the excitement and the fear you experienced when you were caught in a storm.


    **OR**


6.  **Write a short story** using **ONE** of the following titles:

    Stormchaser              Lightning Strikes Twice.


    **OR**


7.  **Write a newspaper article** with the following headline:

    Storm Causes Widespread Damage.


    **OR**


8.  Weather plays an important part in our everyday lives.
    **Give your views.**


**[Turn over**

FIRST    **Look at the picture opposite.**
         **It shows a group of students.**

NEXT     Think about life during and after school.

WHAT YOU HAVE TO WRITE

9.    **Giving reasons**, write about your plans for when you leave school.

      **OR**

10.   **Write a short story** using the following title:

      The Examination.

      **OR**

11.   **Write an article** for your school magazine in which you describe the high points **and** the low points of your school years.

      **OR**

12.   New places, new faces.

      **Write about** a time when you had to cope with new people in new surroundings.

      Remember to include your **thoughts and feelings**.

                                                                    **[Turn over**

FIRST    **Look at the picture opposite.**
         **It shows a traffic jam.**

NEXT     Think about travel problems.

---

| WHAT YOU HAVE TO WRITE |
| --- |

---

13. **Write about** an occasion when you were delayed during a journey.
    You should concentrate on your **thoughts and feelings**.


    **OR**


14. **Write a short story** using the following title:
    The Road to Nowhere.


    **OR**


15. Road rage, air rage—the modern age.
    Life today is simply too stressful.
    **Discuss.**


**[Turn over**

FIRST      **Look at the picture opposite.
           It shows a young couple who have fallen out.**

NEXT       Think about relationships.

---
| WHAT YOU HAVE TO WRITE |
---

16. **Write a short story** using **ONE** of the following openings:

    **EITHER**

    Jill stared ahead intently, always away from him, focused firmly on the wall.  He tried to speak.  She raised her arm in protest . . .

    **OR**

    Andrew didn't know what to do.  Just hours earlier things had been simply perfect.  Now this.  He let his mind wander back to . . .


    **OR**


17. Magazines for young people do more good than harm.

    **Give your views.**


    **OR**


18. **Write about** your **thoughts and feelings** at a time when you were aware that someone simply wasn't listening.


**[Turn over for assignments 19 to 21 on *Page twelve***

**There are no pictures for these assignments.**

19. **Write a short story** using the following opening.

"He awoke in the ashes of a dead city. The cruel sun glared, showing neither pity nor mercy. He shook himself. It was no dream."

Make sure that you develop **character** and **setting** as well as **plot**.

**OR**

20. Look at me!

Is it more important to be an individual or to fit in with the crowd?

**Discuss.**

**OR**

21. **Write a short story** using the title:

Out of Time.

Make sure that you develop **character** and **setting** as well as **plot**.

*[END OF QUESTION PAPER]*

STANDARD GRADE | FOUNDATION | GENERAL | CREDIT

# 2007
## WRITING

[BLANK PAGE]

**F**
**G**
**C**

# 0860/407

NATIONAL
QUALIFICATIONS
2007

TUESDAY, 1 MAY
9.00 AM – 10.15 AM

ENGLISH
STANDARD GRADE
Foundation, General
and Credit Levels
Writing

**Read This First**

1   Inside this booklet, there are photographs and words.
Use them to help you when you are thinking about what to write.
Look at all the material and think about all the possibilities.

2   There are 23 assignments altogether for you to choose from.

3   Decide which assignment you are going to attempt.
Choose only **one** and write its number in the margin of your answer book.

4   Pay close attention to what you are asked to write.
**Plan** what you are going to write.
Read and check your work before you hand it in.
Any changes to your work should be made clearly.

SCOTTISH
QUALIFICATIONS
AUTHORITY

©

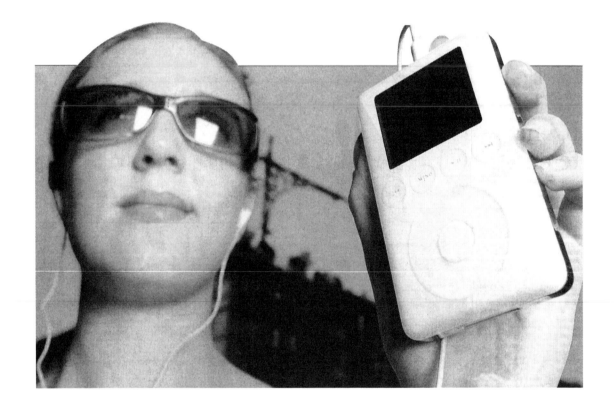

FIRST          **Look at the picture opposite.**
               **It shows a young woman with an MP3 player.**


NEXT           Think about the importance of technology.

---
WHAT YOU HAVE TO WRITE
---

1. The one piece of technology I couldn't live without.

   **Write about** the importance to you of **ONE** piece of technology.


   **OR**


2. Young people today care too much for personal possessions.

   **Give your views.**


   **OR**


3. **Write a short story** using **ONE** of the following titles:

   Futureshock                      She Saw the Future.

   You should develop **setting** and **character** as well as **plot**.


                                                        **[Turn over**

FIRST     **Look at the picture opposite.**
                 **It shows a young boy being led by his mother.**

NEXT     Think about your schooldays.

---

WHAT YOU HAVE TO WRITE

---

4. School Memories.

   **Write about** a person, place, or incident from your schooldays which you find unforgettable.

   Remember to include your **thoughts and feelings**.

   **OR**

5. **Write a short story** using the following opening:

   The reluctance was written all over John's face. He tugged at his mother's hand. He winced. He grimaced. He complained. Still his mother led him on . . .

   You should develop **setting** and **character** as well as **plot**.

   **OR**

6. All pupils should wear school uniform.

   **Give your views.**

   **[Turn over**

FIRST        **Look at the picture opposite.**
             **It shows a lake in winter.**


NEXT         Think about special places.

---

| WHAT YOU HAVE TO WRITE |
| --- |

7.  Sometimes a special place can inspire us.

    **Write about** such a place.

    Remember to include your **thoughts and feelings**.


    **OR**


8.  **Write in any way you choose** using the picture opposite as your inspiration.


    **OR**


9.  **Write about** a time when you were alone but happy.

    You should concentrate on your **thoughts and feelings**.


    **OR**


10. **Write an informative article** for a travel magazine titled:

    The Best Holiday Destination For Young People.


**[Turn over**

FIRST     **Look at the picture opposite.**
               **It shows a man under pressure.**

NEXT     Think about the pressures of life.

---

### WHAT YOU HAVE TO WRITE

11. **Write about** a time in your life when you had to face personal pressure.

    You should describe your **thoughts and feelings**.

    **OR**

12. **Write a short story** using **ONE** of the following titles:

    The Underdog                    Free at Last.

    You should develop **setting** and **character** as well as **plot**.

    **OR**

13. It's Just Not Fair!

    **Write about** an occasion when you took a stand against injustice.

    You should concentrate on your **thoughts and feelings** as well as what you did.

    **OR**

14. These days young people are unfairly treated by the media.

    **Give your views.**

    **[Turn over**

FIRST          **Look at the picture opposite.**
               **It shows a young woman on a bus, alone with her thoughts.**

NEXT           Think about moments of reflection.

---

| WHAT YOU HAVE TO WRITE |
| :--- |

15. "The glass is always half full; never half empty."

    It is important to have a positive outlook on life.

    **Give your views.**

    **OR**

16. **Write about** an occasion when you had an unpleasant duty to perform.

    You should concentrate on your **thoughts and feelings**.

    **OR**

17. Act Your Age!

    There are fewer chances today simply to be yourself.

    **Give your views.**

    **OR**

18. **Write a short story** using **ONE** of the following titles:

    Stranger in a Strange Land                    No Return.

    You should develop **setting** and **character** as well as **plot**.

    **[Turn over for assignments 19 to 23 on *Page twelve***

**There are no pictures for these assignments.**

19. We should try to solve the problems here on earth before we spend more on space exploration.

    **Give your views.**

    **OR**

20. **Describe the scene** brought to mind by the following:

    A stark land of leafless trees and merciless wind.

    **OR**

21. We forget our past at our peril!

    Not enough is being done to keep Scottish heritage alive.

    **Write a newspaper article** in which you give your views on this topic.

    **OR**

22. There are special times of the year when people celebrate in their own way.

    **Describe** such a special time, bringing out its importance to you, your family, and your community.

    **OR**

23. **Write a short story** using the following title:

    The Traveller.

    You should develop **setting** and **character** as well as **plot**.

*[END OF QUESTION PAPER]*

# 2008
## WRITING

[BLANK PAGE]

**F
G
C**

# 0860/407

NATIONAL
QUALIFICATIONS
2008

TUESDAY, 6 MAY
9.00 AM – 10.15 AM

ENGLISH
STANDARD GRADE
Foundation, General
and Credit Levels
Writing

### Read This First

1    Inside this booklet, there are photographs and words.
Use them to help you when you are thinking about what to write.
Look at all the material and think about all the possibilities.

2    There are 22 assignments altogether for you to choose from.

3    Decide which assignment you are going to attempt.
Choose only **one** and write its number in the margin of your answer book.

4    Pay close attention to what you are asked to write.
**Plan** what you are going to write.
Read and check your work before you hand it in.
Any changes to your work should be made clearly.

FIRST **Look at the picture opposite.**
**It shows a car in heavy rain and hail.**

NEXT Think about the dangers of extreme weather.

WHAT YOU HAVE TO WRITE

1. **Write a short story** using the following opening:

   The car skidded violently. He struggled to regain control. Close to panic, he wrenched the steering wheel to the right . . .

   You should develop **setting** and **character** as well as **plot**.

   **OR**

2. What's going on with our weather?

   Individuals need to take steps to tackle climate change.

   **Give your views.**

   **OR**

3. Journeys can take unexpected turns.

   **Write about** an occasion when this happened to **you**.

   Remember to include your **thoughts and feelings**.

   **[Turn over**

FIRST     **Look at the picture opposite.**
          **It shows young people together in a school cafeteria.**

NEXT      Think about school experiences.

---

| WHAT YOU HAVE TO WRITE |
| --- |

4.  A Best Friend Should Be . . .

    **Write about** the ideal qualities of a best friend.


    **OR**


5.  Youth culture.  There's no such thing.

    **Give your views**.


    **OR**


6.  **Write about** an occasion when your loyalty to a friend was pushed to the limit.

    Remember to include your **thoughts and feelings**.


    **OR**


7.  **Write a short story** using the following title:

    The School Gate.

    You should develop **setting** and **character** as well as **plot**.


                                                              **[Turn over**

FIRST      **Look at the picture opposite.**
                 **It shows a man staring.**

NEXT      Think about being observed.

> WHAT YOU HAVE TO WRITE

8.  Big Brother is Watching You!

    **Write about** an occasion when you felt that there was no escape from authority.

    Remember to include your **thoughts and feelings**.

    **OR**

9.  **Write a short story** using **ONE** of the following titles:

    Seeing is Believing              Close Up

    You should develop **setting** and **character** as well as **plot**.

    **OR**

10. All You Need is an Audience.

    The media give young people the idea that success comes easily.

    **Give your views**.

**[Turn over**

FIRST **Look at the picture opposite.**
**It shows a boy with his grandfather.**

NEXT Think about the positive relationship you have with an older relative.

---

## WHAT YOU HAVE TO WRITE

11. **Write about** an occasion when you learned a valuable lesson from an older relative.

    Remember to include your **thoughts and feelings**.

    **OR**

12. **Write a short story** using the following opening:

    Those were the moments he loved most. Grandpa reading to him with that lilting voice telling stories of . . .

    You should develop **setting** and **character** as well as **plot**.

    **OR**

13. We do not give the older generation the respect they deserve.
    **Give your views**.

    **OR**

14. **Write in any way you choose** using the picture opposite as your inspiration.

**[Turn over**

FIRST **Look at the picture opposite.**
**It shows an aircraft in the sunset.**

NEXT Think about air travel.

---

WHAT YOU HAVE TO WRITE

---

15. The damage to the environment caused by aircraft outweighs the advantages of cheap air travel.

    **Give your views**.

    **OR**

16. **Write a short story** using **ONE** of the following titles:

    A New Beginning          Touchdown

    You should develop **setting** and **character** as well as **plot**.

    **OR**

17. **Write in any way you choose** using the picture opposite as your inspiration.

[**Turn over for assignments 18 to 22 on *Page twelve***

**There are no pictures for these assignments.**

18. **Write an informative article** for your school magazine titled:

    Technology: the impact on my education.

    **OR**

19. Nowadays there is less freedom of choice.

    **Give your views**.

    **OR**

20. **Write a short story** with the following opening:

    Beth stared again at the square glow from the computer screen in disbelief. She was going to be reunited with her sister at long last. She could hardly wait . . .

    You should develop **setting** and **character** as well as **plot**.

    **OR**

21. Education is about what we learn both **inside** and **outside** the classroom.

    **Give your views**.

    **OR**

22. **Describe the scene** brought to mind by **ONE** of the following:
    **EITHER**

    Snow fell, the flimsiest drops of geometric perfection, lightly, gently onto the village rooftops.

    **OR**

    With merciless rage, the sun scorched the earth to brittle hardness.

*[END OF QUESTION PAPER]*

# STANDARD GRADE | FOUNDATION | GENERAL | CREDIT

# 2009
## WRITING

[BLANK PAGE]

**F**
**G**
**C**

# 0860/407

NATIONAL
QUALIFICATIONS
2009

FRIDAY, 8 MAY
9.00 AM – 10.15 AM

ENGLISH
STANDARD GRADE
Foundation, General
and Credit Levels
Writing

### Read This First

1   Inside this booklet, there are photographs and words.
    Use them to help you when you are thinking about what to write.
    Look at all the material and think about all the possibilities.

2   There are 21 assignments altogether for you to choose from.

3   Decide which assignment you are going to attempt.
    Choose only **one** and write its number in the margin of your answer book.

4   Pay close attention to what you are asked to write.
    **Plan** what you are going to write.
    Read and check your work before you hand it in.
    Any changes to your work should be made clearly.

FIRST    **Look at the picture opposite.**
         **It shows a statue overlooking a city.**

NEXT    Think about life in a city.

---

| WHAT YOU HAVE TO WRITE |
| --- |

1. **Write about an occasion** when you went on a school trip to a city.

   Remember to include your **thoughts and feelings**.


   **OR**


2. Holidays are not just about sun, sea and sand.

   **Give your views.**


   **OR**


3. **Write a short story** using the following opening:

   From a great height he watched.  Cars, buses, boats, people. Slowly, he drew his plans . . .

   You should develop **setting** and **character** as well as **plot**.


   **OR**


4. **Write in any way you choose** using the picture opposite as your inspiration.


**[Turn over**

FIRST      **Look at the pictures opposite.**
**They show people involved in different sports.**

NEXT      Think about what sport means to you.

---

WHAT YOU HAVE TO WRITE

---

5. My Sporting Hero.

   **Write a magazine article** giving information about your favourite sportsperson.

   **OR**

6. There should be more opportunities for sport in local communities.

   **Give your views**.

   **OR**

7. **Write a short story** using the title:

   Against the Odds

   You should develop **setting** and **character** as well as **plot**.

   **OR**

8. **Write about** a sporting occasion when taking part was more important than winning.

   Remember to include your **thoughts and feelings**.

**[Turn over**

FIRST      **Look at the picture opposite.**
                   **It shows a tigress and her cubs.**

NEXT      Think about protecting animals.

---

WHAT YOU HAVE TO WRITE

---

9. One of the Family.

   **Write about** the importance of a pet in your life.

   Remember to include your **thoughts and feelings**.

   **OR**

10. **Write a magazine article** in which you present the case **for** the protection of an animal in danger.

    **OR**

11. **Write a short story** using **ONE** of the following titles:

    The Animal Kingdom       Animal Magic

    You should develop **setting** and **character** as well as **plot**.

    **[Turn over**

FIRST      **Look at the picture opposite.**
**It shows a man at the top of a staircase.**

NEXT      Think about achievements in your life.

---

| WHAT YOU HAVE TO WRITE |
| --- |

12. **Write about** an occasion when you achieved a personal goal after a struggle.

    Remember to include your **thoughts and feelings**.

    **OR**

13. Achievement in school is about more than success in exams.

    **Give your views**.

    **OR**

14. **Write a short story** using the following opening:

    It had been tough. Sacrifice. Time. Effort. Now she had succeeded. Let the new life begin . . .

    You should develop **setting** and **character** as well as **plot**.

**[Turn over**

FIRST      **Look at the picture opposite.**
                **It shows two people on a survival course.**

NEXT      Think about outdoor activities.

---

WHAT YOU HAVE TO WRITE

---

15. **Write about** an occasion when you learned new skills through taking part in an outdoor activity.

    Remember to include your **thoughts and feelings**.

    **OR**

16. **Write a short story** using the following title:

    Trapped in the Forest

    You should develop **setting** and **character** as well as **plot**.

    **OR**

17. Outdoor education should be available to all pupils.

    **Give your views**.

**[Turn over for assignments 18 to 21 on *Page twelve***

**There are no pictures for these assignments.**

18. **Describe the scene** brought to mind by **ONE** of the following:

    Light as air, they hovered then swooped, twisting impossibly around feather clouds.

    **OR**

    Waves lapped at pebbles on the distant shore and a kindly sun drew a gentle haze over the land.

19. Holidays at home are better for the environment than going abroad.

    **Give your views**.

    **OR**

20. **Write about** an occasion when you were a positive role model for a friend or relative.

    Remember to include your **thoughts and feelings**.

    **OR**

21. **Write a short story** using the following title:

    Paradise Lost

    You should develop **setting** and **character** as well as **plot**.

*[END OF QUESTION PAPER]*

[BLANK PAGE]

[BLANK PAGE]

[BLANK PAGE]

# Acknowledgements

Permission has been sought from all relevant copyright holders and Bright Red Publishing is grateful for the use of the following:

A photograph © Corey Rich/Aurora Photos (2006 Foundation Close Reading page 2);

An article adapted from 'Ain't no mountain high enough' by Deborah Netburn, taken from the Sunday Telegraph Magazine, © Telegraph Media Group Limited (27 June 2004) (2006 Foundation Close Reading page 2);

Extract from 'You Don't Know Me' by David Klass. Reprinted with permission from The Aaron M. Priest Literary Agency, 2009 (2006 General Close Reading pages 2 & 3);

A photograph of lightning taken from www.sydneystormchasers.com © James Harris (2006 F/G/C Writing page 4);

The photograph, 'Scots will be squeezed out. "Fee Refugees!"' by David Moir, taken from The Scotsman, 26 August 2004 © The Scotsman Publications Ltd (2006 F/G/C Writing page 6);

The photograph, 'Stretching the Nerves' by Kieran Dodds © Herald & Times Group (2006 F/G/C Writing page 8);

The photograph 'People' © Design Pics/Alamy Limited (2006 F/G/C Writing page 10);

The article 'Why dumped dog is such a lucky hound' by David Wigg and pictures by Douglas Morrison © The Sunday Express (2007 Foundation Close Reading pages 2 & 3);

Article adapted from 'The Fabulous Biker Boys (and Girls)' by John Dodd taken from the Sunday Telegraph Magazine © Telegraph Media Group (28 August 2005) (2007 General Close Reading page 2);

The photograph, 'iPod Generation' © Dan Callister/RexFeatures (2007 F/G/C Writing page 2);

A photograph © Hulton Archive/Getty (2007 F/G/C Writing page 4);

A photograph © www.danheller.com (2007 F/G/C Writing page 6);

A picture © Hashim Akib (2007 F/G/C Writing page 8);

A photograph © David Hogsholt/Reportage by Getty Images (2007 F/G/C Writing page 10);

An extract from 'Home for Christmas' taken from a book called 'Mysterious Christmas Tales' by David Belbin. Published by Scholastic. Reproduced with permission of Jennifer Luithlen Agency (2008 Foundation Close Reading pages 2 & 3);

The article 'Saddle the white horses' by Dave Flanagan, taken from The Herald magazine 22 April 2006 (2008 General Close Reading page 2);

A photograph taken from www.bigfoto.com (2008 F/G/C Writing page 2);

The photograph 'Chips are down' by Robert Perry taken from Scotland on Sunday, 2 July 2006 © The Scotsman Publications Ltd (2008 F/G/C Writing page 4);

The photograph 'Eye Opener' © Steve Double (2008 F/G/C Writing page 6);

The photograph 'Airbus 320' by Ian Britton. Reproduced with permission of Freefoto.com (2008 F/G/C Writing page 10);

An extract from 'Crocodile River' by Geoffrey Malone, published by Hodder Children's Books (2000) (2009 Foundation Close Reading pages 2 & 3);

An extract from 'Labyrinth' by Kate Mosse, published by Orion Books (2005) (2009 General Close Reading pages 2 & 3);

A photograph taken from www.bigfoto.com (2009 F/G/C Writing page 2);

A photograph © FRANCK FIFE/AFP/Getty Images (2009 F/G/C Writing page 4);

A photograph by Phil Wilkinson © The Scotsman Publications Ltd (2009 F/G/C Writing page 4);

The photograph 'Surfing. Saltburn by the Sea, Yorkshire' by Ian Britton. Reproduced with permission of Freefoto.com (2009 F/G/C Writing page 4);

A photograph of a girl ski-ing © Neil McQuoid (2009 F/G/C Writing page 4);

The photograph, 'Supermum Tigress licks her new cubs in Hongshan Zoo in Nanjing, China' © Herald & Times Group (2009 F/G/C Writing page 6);

A photograph © Blackout Concepts/Alamy (2009 F/G/C Writing page 8);

The photograph 'I will survive: Learning to make fire without matches is a basic bushcraft skill © Roger Bamber/Alamy (2009 F/G/C Writing page 10).